REVIEWS FOR
MIRACLES IN MY LIFE

It has been said, if you read a book worth reading, the message of that book, will stay with you forever. *Miracles In My Life* is one of those books. "Charlie," is really, an everyman kind of guy. He is very comfortable and open in telling you his story as you will see from page one. *Miracles In My Life* is memorable, relatable, warmly encouraging, and one that will leave you hopeful, and thankful to Our Father in Heaven, for His gracious, loving, caring and guiding work in your own life. What happened to Charlie Hunt, is still happening, and it's my prayer, that this book will encourage you to trust in our Faithful God and Savior Jesus Christ all the more, or perhaps for the first time. It has been said, "He is there. And He is not silent." You will find Him, and hear Him throughout this book.

—Pastor Bob Grenier, Calvary Chapel, Visalia, CA

What a journey! From an aimless hippie in the Seventies to a photographer's helper to an electrical engineer at a world-class university. In this remarkable autobiography – a quick and fascinating read – Hunt looks back on his life's astonishing twists and turns and describes the miracles large and small that guided him from start to finish – unmistakably orchestrated by the Holy Spirit.

—**Michael Guillen, PhD**, *Physicist, bestselling author, Emmy-winning journalist, and host of "Science + God with Dr. G"*

Anyone who reads the Bible knows that God did miracles in Bible times, but it's always good to hear of how God is working today. As you read *Miracles In My Life*, you'll be thankful that God still works mightily and miraculously in the lives of those who trust Him. Hearing how God has worked in the life of Charles Hunt will encourage you to trust God to work in your life.

—**David Guzik**, *Pastor and Author of the widely-used Enduring Word Bible Commentary*

I was deeply moved and my faith was strengthened when I had the honor of reading Professor Hunt's manuscript. In my view, the three central components of a maturing Christian life involve the life of the mind, spiritual and inner transformation, and experiencing miracles and other forms of God's manifest Presence. But we Westerners are too skeptical of the miraculous. What we need are credible, eyewitness accounts of signs and wonders to build our own expectation. Professor Hunt's book is exactly the sort of thing we need in our time, and I urge you to read it and get copies for your friends. You won't regret it.

—**JP Moreland,** *Distinguished Professor of Philosophy, Talbot School of Theology and author of Finding Quiet.*

***

Why won't God make Himself known to me? God's hiddenness keeps some people from faith and troubles others who have put their trust in the person of Christ. In this inspiring and deeply personal work, Charles Hunt reminds us that God is close and ever-present for those who have eyes to see. And the evidence for God's ongoing involvement in our lives are the miracles and wonders all around us—both big and small. Through an autobiographical recounting of the miracles he has experienced in his life, Charles Hunt helps us clearly see how God has directed the steps of his life, giving us hope that He will do the same for each of us.

—**Fazale 'Fuz' Rana, PhD**, *Vice President of Research and Apologetics, Reasons to Believe*

MIRACLES IN MY LIFE

by

CHARLES E. HUNT

DEDICATION

Now, as then, the most beautiful girl I've ever seen. My Carla. "But of all God's miracles large and small, the most miraculous one of all, is the one I thought could never be: God has given you to me."

FRONT COVER

Cathedral Peak in Yosemite National Park. The right edge in the picture shows the Southeast Buttress, which is the location described in the first chapter, Part Zero.

TABLE OF CONTENTS

Dedication   vii

Acknowledgement   xi

Preface   xiii

Part Zero

Climbing Cathedral Peak in Yosemite   17

Part One

Revelation, Keith, Rodney, Bob, And the Book of Life 24

Holy Ghost   33

Sin in The Red House   38

That Girl   40

Two Bandanas And Temptation   43

Jan At the Aronos Club   46

The Least in The Kingdom   49

My Fleece   52

Part Two

The Comfort I Never Expected   57

Slain   61

Did Jesus Really Die and Forgive All Our Sins? 65

I Saw Jesus   **69**

Having Our First Son   **77**

The Guys with The Gimpy Legs   **79**

Michaelino's Italian Restaurant   **86**

Shining the Light or Casting Out Darkness   **90**

Time to Leave: It's in His Hands   **94**

Part Three

A Pillar of Peace   **99**

Shaking the President's Hand   **104**

Part Four

The Giant Snowball   **107**

My Father In Heaven   **110**

The Three Palms   **118**

The Sting of a Lifetime   **124**

A Dark Day Behind the Barn   **127**

The Holy Mountain   **129**

The Messenger In The Airport   **132**

How Noma Died   **137**

Was Blind But Now I See   **139**

Afterword   **145**

ACKNOWLEDGEMENT

First of all, I thank my youngest daughter, Lila, for inspiring me and encouraging me to write this book. I thank Pastor John Davis, Prof. JP Moreland, David Keane and Pastor Sumit Sen for their constructive criticisms and encouragement. Most especially, I thank Pastor Bob Grenier, who has been my Chief Protagonist from start to finish. Blessings to you all!

PREFACE

Here are some miracles I've experienced in my life.

Author, Eric Metaxas, astutely asked, "If a miracle happens in the woods, and there's no one around to see it, is it a miracle?" The fact is, there are miracles all around us, and we typically don't see them. The Lord performed miracles to catch peoples' attention.

> *But if I with the finger of God cast out devils, no doubt the kingdom of God is come upon you.*
> Luke 11:20

Jesus didn't walk this world as some genie who got out of the bottle. His miracles were a tool He used so people would believe His words and be saved from their sins. But there were times when people wanted Jesus to perform a miracle and He intentionally chose not to, seeing that it would bear no fruit. Even if He had done the miraculous for them, they would not have believed His gospel; and He perceived that.

Innumerable miracles have occurred through Jesus' disciples, both while He walked the earth, and since His ascension to heaven. His objectives, however, haven't changed. These events happened in their presence, in them, and through them. And so it continues to this day.

Some miracles were events which could be ascribed to natural occurrences. Deathly-sick people recover and are restored to health; it happens at times. But when Jesus walked into the room where someone laid dying, prayed, and that person rose up immediately to health: that's a miracle.

Some miracles had natural consequences; but clearly could not happen. People sit on the grass for a picnic most every week. But when Jesus told five thousand people to sit, and kept reaching into the same picnic basket, filled with lunch for one, and pulled out a picnic for all of them: that's a miracle.

Some miracles clearly defy the laws of physics. Jesus walked on water. Jesus called into the tomb of Lazarus, who had died four days before, "Come out!" Lazarus, bound in his burial wrappings, hobbled out—alive.

Most importantly, having foretold His followers that the worst would happen, Jesus submitted to being crucified by the Romans. They watched Him die and buried Him. Three days later, He resurrected to life in a glorified, immortal body. That's THE miracle. We have eternal hope because He promised that if we believe Him, our sins will be forgiven, and we will also rise to eternal life.

Hundreds of years before the birth of Jesus, the prophet, Daniel, noted that even the pagan Babylonian king, Nebuchadnezzar, exclaimed:

How great are his miracles, and how mighty
his wonders! His kingdom is an eternal kingdom,
and his dominion is from generation to generation.
Daniel 4:3

There is nothing in the Scriptures to insinuate that God has ever stopped performing miracles, or ever will. In fact, it's clear to me that He hasn't changed at all. Miracles and wonders persist and are all around us. We can see them if we pay attention. Since I became a Believer in Jesus at twenty-one years old, I have experienced and witnessed many miracles. They weren't things which converted me to become a Believer; but they have strengthened my faith, taught me lessons, and convinced me that Our Father and His Son, Jesus, really love me and those around me.

The stories I relate here are true. C.S. Lewis said, "Memory, once waked, will play the tyrant." God help me that it doesn't happen here. I gave careful thought to assure I'm not embellishing things, nor manipulating facts. Most everyone mentioned is given their real names because I want to honor my heroes. A few are given pseudonyms because I don't intend to shame the guilty. And one or two minor participants are given a fictitious name, merely because I can't remember their real names

PART ZERO

CLIMBING CATHEDRAL PEAK IN YOSEMITE

I dropped out of college after my sophomore year. It wasn't because I wasn't doing well or didn't find classes interesting. I simply had no direction or vision in my life. It was the height of the Hippie Era, and I was living in San Francisco. From one perspective, I was in the center of the Universe and all the Earth was in flux because of what we perceived was happening.

From another vantage point, it was emptiness and futility. Beyond our façade of Peace, Love, Freedom and Openness, there was virtually no substance. It wasn't even clear who "we" were. There was no leadership, no objective, no identity, and no purpose. It's unlikely I could have articulated what I felt inside of me at the time; but I realized everything I was doing was ultimately worthless. It's hard to be motivated when you feel that way. It was fertile ground for narcissism and nihilism.

A job opened in Yosemite working for the concessionaire, Curry Company, in the dining room of the famous Ahwahnee Hotel. My high school friend, Dave, had applied. After his immediate hire, he was told, "Invite your friends to apply. We need people." So he contacted me and I followed in his path. I made very good money there, for a nineteen-year-old kid in 1972. It was all young people and spectacular surroundings. Cleaning up and cutting my hair was a small price to pay.

I eventually worked for the National Park Service as a "park aide." I was the guy who made reservations, collected camping site fees, and told the masses where the nearest restroom was. It wasn't until May, 1974 that I became a Believer in Jesus; but the intervening years were the best and the worst.

I was a very lonely boy. I made good grades but was only modest at sports. I never learned how to appropriately give place to other peoples' feelings and perspectives. Coming from a line of over-educated ancestors (including my high-powered grandfather, the attorney) I could out-argue almost anybody on just about any topic. None of this constituted the best building material for making friends.

When I began working in Yosemite, I not only had the attraction of the natural surroundings, but there were lots of fellow employees with common interests— many of whom were attractive girls. I had never had a girlfriend and I hoped this was my chance. I was not overly appealing to girls. I hadn't quite figured out that you generally make more friends being good to folks, as opposed to trying to impress them.

Yosemite is the world's greatest place for rock climbing and I quickly learned. My acquaintances, who were expert rock climbers, had all the girls around them. It hadn't dawned on me that the attraction was not necessarily their climbing technique. But it was an easy way to make friends because you can't climb the rocks alone; everybody needed climbing partners.

I could do the regular, established routes in the park. I could even lead on a pitch which meant climbing out ahead, setting the protection, and looping the rope through a carabiner at the end of the protection. While I led the pitch—which extended about the full 150-foot length of the rope—my partner would be at the bottom of that pitch, keeping the rope tight and being "on belay" in case I fell. I had fallen once or twice; but never far, and I had never hurt myself. My belaying partners always did their job well. We all held great respect for the sheer cliffs we were climbing.

I was not, however, always very accepting of my own limitations. My desire to do something challenging on the rocks was itching. If I completed something impressive on the rocks, surely, I'd dazzle the girls, right? One summer day, I went with my fairly-novice, climbing buddy, Roy, up to Tuolumne Meadows and Cathedral Peak. I had decided we would climb the Southeast Buttress. This is an established, long climb of six pitches, considered only moderately hard. I had never climbed the Southeast Buttress but my climbing buddies had told me it was easy to spot the route and that I should be able to do it. The route in question is surrounded by much harder climbs, all in the 5-9 range, or more. That morning, Roy and I hiked from the meadow up to the base of what was clearly the route we wanted.

Silly me. I had neglected to factor in three important issues before I climbed out in the lead. First, I had never led this long of a climb before and didn't realize how tiring such a vertical climbing task is, especially at base elevation of 12,000 feet. I also was not as strong as my expert climbing buddies; although it's unlikely I would have admitted that. Finally, Roy was not sufficiently experienced to lead and set protection, so I had to lead every pitch. This meant I had no back-up if I got in trouble.

The first four pitches of the climb went reasonably well but I was very tired. On the fifth pitch, I couldn't really tell where I was going and I went up the wrong crack. As I went higher, the crack continued to get smaller and was very hard to use. I set protection and looped the rope through; but I was about seventy feet above Roy. On I went, but the crack got smaller and smaller; finally, about twenty-five feet above my last protection, the crack completely ended. There was nothing but bare rock above me, or around me. There was nothing to grab onto. At this point of the Buttress, it was extreme and near vertical. There was no possibility to climb back down. I was not happy.

In my awful feeling of desperation, I looked to my left. I could see the crack of my intended route, about eight feet away. My one leg dangled free; the other was crammed at an angle below me in the last of the crack I had taken. It was all that supported my weight. I started to experience what all climbers dread: sewing machine leg. This is the oscillation in your muscles, right before things give way. If I fell from there, I would drop to fifty feet below, at which point—if my last protection held and Roy could withstand the jolt of my fall—the rope would catch me and Roy could lower me down. The more-pressing problem was that if I fell that far on Yosemite's jagged granite, it would turn me into human hamburger, if I even survived.

At that point in my life, I was not following Jesus. I'm not sure I really believed there was a God. However, desperation does tend to bring us to praying, even if we don't know Who it is we're praying to. My prayer was simple, *Oh God! Don't let me die on this stinking rock!. Help me!* I also distinctly remember thinking, *Why did I come up here to climb this? I'm not enjoying it. Roy's not a close friend. If I die, or if I tear myself to shreds and live, hardly anybody will care.*

Right then, I noticed as far out to my left as I could almost reach, a "chicken head." This is a quartz crystal protruding from the granite. Crystals don't erode as fast as the surrounding rock, so chicken heads poke out here and there. This one was about an inch long, about a half-inch around, and slightly pointing up. Some expert climbers might use a chicken head to drape a nylon loop over and use the loop as protection; but you can't fasten to a chicken head, so the loop can slip off. I had never tried such a stunt. I took a loop and a carabiner from my shoulder harness and put the rope through it. I tossed the loop over the chicken head several times until I finally snagged it.

Roy was getting very nervous. "What the heck are you doing? Are you okay?"

My panic-toned bark in response was, "No, I'm not okay! I'm on the brink of falling! When I say the word, gently put tension on the rope so that the chicken head holds me. I'm going to trapeze over to that crack."

Pretending you're Tarzan, using a nylon rope draped from a rock at 12,700 feet above sea level, is not recommended. I did not give Roy the option to discuss my idea. One second later, I yelled, "Tension!" and away I sailed to the left, swinging past the chicken head and over to the crack which I grabbed with vigor. I would have crammed my entire body into the crack, had it been big enough. I was safe. Well, kind of. I didn't fall. I didn't give thanks to God.

Idiots don't change quickly and I am no exception. Acting as though I had any skill at all, I climbed to the nearest ledge and attached myself securely to the rock. I belayed Roy up, as he climbed the correct route. "I'm sorry, Charlie, but I don't see how you did that. It didn't make sense. You are so *lucky* you didn't kill yourself!"

I acted appropriately cool, but inside, I was terrified. After I led the last pitch to the top, we scurried down the trail on the west side back to Tuolumne Meadows for water, food, rest, and solid ground. I only climbed twice more after that. I realized I don't really like rock climbing.

God takes care of us, even when we are in mortal danger and we don't even realize it. It was over a year later when I first read:

> *No harm will come to you; no plague will come near your tent.*
> *For he will give his angels orders concerning you, to protect you in all your ways.*
> *They will support you with their hands so that you will not strike your foot against a stone.*
> Psalm 91:10-12

When I read these words, I remembered Cathedral Peak. I thanked him then

PART ONE

REVELATION, KEITH, RODNEY AND BOB, AND THE BOOK OF LIFE

When I was living in Yosemite, my older brother, John, moved to Sonora, California where he found work. While he was there, he met some Christians who encouraged him to become a Believer. In fact, he did give his life to Jesus. He was a Vietnam veteran, severely injured in the war during the height of the Tet Offensive. When our family heard he had come to faith, we were all terribly condescending and mused amongst ourselves, "Oh, that's good for him. He needs something like that." Of course, we didn't believe that we also *needed something like that.*

I really knew virtually nothing about the Bible, Jesus, or faith. I self-righteously consoled myself with the notion that I believed in God, but any form of god would do for me. I didn't imagine there is Truth.

When I was a kid, I went with my mother to the Episcopal Church and attended Sunday School. We heard a few verses and stories from the Bible. Nobody ever suggested to me that Jesus had died on the cross so that all my sins could be forgiven. It was just religion. I quit going when I turned sixteen, mostly because the priest at the local congregation did not have anything spiritual that I wanted. I identified more with the hippies than with Jesus. One of my friends, Phil, had dabbled in the Jehovah's Witness religion because his parents were a part of that group. Though I doubt Phil believed much of what the Jehovah's Witnesses said, he sometimes talked about things in the Bible: Armageddon, Revelation, and end times. I didn't know anything about these topics except that these things were controversial.

After graduation in 1970, I left high school in Sutter Creek, in the Sierra foothills and headed for the Bay Area. This was the happening place for hippies and that culture. I got a fast-food summer job and rented a basement room from my grade-school principal, Mr. Venter. This was a generous offer to tie me over until the dormitory at San Francisco State opened up in September.

The room was dingy and had only a single, small window but it was very cheap. The walls were lined with the family's old books. I spent a great deal of time that summer reading and listening to music on my record player—and feeling very lonely. One night, having spent the evening attending a rock concert at the famous Fillmore West, I couldn't sleep. I spotted a Bible on the wall and so I decided, thanks to Phil, I'd read the final book of the Bible, Revelation and get acquainted. It was sheer confusion but I finished reading it before dawn. The only thing I read and understood that night, and remember to this day, was in Revelation chapters 20-21. It was about The Lamb's

Book of Life; all the Righteous have their names written in it. This was a wild concept to me, and I remember thinking what a wonderful idea it was the writers of the Bible had dreamt up. I love a crazy story, like *Alice In Wonderland*.

Years later, I would visit John in Sonora. Before he went to Viet Nam, we hadn't been close; but after his horrific injuries, my heart went out to him and we became friends. I was concerned about how he might ever find his way in this world. Though I don't think I ever gave any thought to how I might find *my* way.

I'd usually hitchhike up to Sonora on my days off. John lived in "The Gold House" which was a house populated with newly-saved Christian guys. On the ground floor, lived Keith and his wife, Laura, who loosely ran the house. John didn't talk to me a great deal about Jesus but Keith would always track me down to engage in a conversation about Jesus, the Bible, and faith. Presuming upon my experience from years before, I imagined that I knew the Bible—or, at least, how things ended up—and I loved to argue.

Keith had fresh ears for my contentious nonsense, or so I fantasized. We sparred numerous times. The last time was on a sunny afternoon in front of the Gold House, as I was about to hitch a ride back to Yosemite. I was arguing about something when Keith suddenly stopped. He stared into my eyes, smiled with a look of love I'd never seen before, and short-circuited my entire thought. He slowly leaned forward, tapped me lightly on my chest, and said, "I can't answer anything you're saying; but you know what? I can see that deep in there, you *really* love Jesus."

What do you say to that? He hadn't played by the rules. I had no answer. I didn't know what to say. A knife plunged through where his finger had just been tapping. I quickly got out onto the highway and caught a ride.

The fellow who picked me up was a cool-looking, bearded hippie, about ten years older than me, driving a beautifully-maintained, green Volkswagen Bug. I told him I wanted to get to Yosemite and he said he'd take me as far as Moccasin, which was about forty minutes down the road towards the park. He had to turn off the highway from there towards Coulterville. He gently smiled as he drove but he said nothing more. On the dashboard in front of me were some cute little cartoon stickers. I quickly realized that all of them had Christian themes. I thought, *Oh no! Keith set me up. This fellow is in cahoots with him. It's a conspiracy!* I didn't say anything for a while, but one sticker really bugged me. It said: Jesus is coming back!

"Do you really believe that?" I asked. He looked somewhat surprised that I had said anything. He didn't really know what I was talking about. I pointed to the unnerving sticker. "Oh. You mean *that*? Well, yes, I do believe it." From that moment on, he talked non-stop all the way to Moccasin. I couldn't say a thing. Hearing him talk was like drinking golden rain drops from Heaven. I didn't know who he was, but I realized that I loved him. And I could really see that he loved

Jesus. For him, it was clear that Jesus is alive and not some legend that the religions talk about.

He dropped me off at the turn-off and I waited for over an hour before anybody came along to give me a ride into the park. I stood there spellbound, looking around. For the first time in my life, I could tell. I'm not alone. I could feel *Him*, as though I was surrounded on all sides. He was right there.

In May 1974, I had the whole month free before the Yosemite summer season started in all its glory. I decided to go visit a high-school friend in Bellingham, Washington. I drove my pickup as far as Eugene, Oregon when I started having engine trouble. The shop guy told me it would be a few days until the part arrived, but that I could drive about locally before things would fail altogether. I decided to find a former roommate of mine who now lived in Eugene. He let me sleep on his floor but we didn't spend any time together. The last time I'd seen him, over a year earlier, he'd told me as he packed for Eugene, "Hey. Any time you're up north in Oregon, stop by and see me." Once I did come to see him, the welcome wasn't warm at all. He felt obligated to at least keep me out of the rain. During the day, I went to the University of Oregon campus to watch the pretty girls but I couldn't get myself to meet any of them; I was too socially awkward.

In the Want Ads of the university paper was this one-liner: Lonely? Call this number. Even though I was far too cool to admit how lonely I was, I wrote down the number anyway, and I called it late that afternoon.

A nice girl's voice answered and I said, "I saw the paper's ad. Yes, I'm lonely." I was hoping this would lead me to a party or some other social event where I could meet someone. She responded, "Well, this is actually a suicide hotline. Are you suicidal?" I wasn't. She went on to say that although she couldn't really help me with my personal loneliness, she could introduce me to her friend, Bob, who she was sure would want to meet me.

"Hold on. I have another line here. I'll call Bob right now." I was feeling funny about this exchange, but I waited. Maybe Bob was having a party. In a second came the charming voice again, "Hello, Charlie? I've got Bob on the line and he says, 'Tell him to come on over.' I think you should go meet him." She gave me the address and I started driving.

It was the evening of May 22. It's hard to explain the funny feeling of driving across a strange town, to go to the house of an unknown somebody named Bob, for some unknown reason. I arrived at this frumpy house in old-town Eugene and walked up the stairs. The door swung open, and there stood a smiling bearded wonder, who said, "Charlie? Come on in!" I walked in feeling quite welcomed. Inside was a living room with a half dozen guys; they were all reading the Bible. I didn't realize then that I had walked into the Shiloh Youth Revival Christian House.

"Whoa. I gotta go!" I swung around and headed to the door. Bob grabbed me by the shoulders and said, "Wait. I just want to ask you one thing. Okay? Do you want to accept Jesus?" He didn't preach to me, or

29

argue, or say anything else. That second, for the first time, life made sense. It was like everything suddenly came into focus: Keith, the VW with the stickers, Brother John, and many other pieces in a giant puzzle. This was a moment that my entire life had been leading towards. I looked Bob straight in the eyes. "Yes. I do."

"You do?"

He had never had anyone say "yes" before.

After scrambling for a moment, Bob took me up into the attic where we were alone. There, he led me in a prayer to ask Jesus into my heart. I knew that, for the first time in my life, I was doing the right thing. After we both said "Amen," Bob came apart at the seams. He raised his arms into the air and started enthusiastically praising God. I'd never seen anything like this before in my life.

"Thank You for saving Charlie! Thank You for letting me be here!" I was elated; but I didn't know what to make of Bob. He went from shouts of praise to tears of joy. He went on and on. Then, just when I was thinking *maybe it's time to get out of here*, Bob suddenly stopped. He got quiet. Then he said, "Yes Lord. I see it. I see that you have just written Charlie's name into *The Lamb's Book of Life*. Praise You!"

Keith's knife thrust through me again. But this time it didn't convict me. This time, it confirmed everything. "I know about that Book!" It's really true. I was stunned.

A few days later, after some wonderful time in Eugene, the pickup was fixed and I decided to get back. I had to be on the job before Memorial Day weekend. Bob strongly advised me not to leave. "You're just a baby Christian. If you leave now, you'll certainly backslide." But I did leave. I'm glad Bob was wrong that time.

Driving along on Sunday, I went through Bend, Oregon. There was a small church by the side of the road. I noticed that people were going in so I stopped and joined them. After the service, the minister came up to me and welcomed me warmly. He asked who I was. I'm pretty sure he hadn't seen many hippies wander in for worship. I told him my story from Eugene and he was amazed. He was very affirming and encouraged me to live for Jesus. Since I didn't have a Bible, he gave me one and he encouraged me in my first habits as a disciple. "Read this book and get to know what it says. And pray. And be part of the Church, wherever you are living." I doubt I understood at the time how profound his encouragement was but I started devouring The Book right away.

The next time I saw Keith, he was My Dear Brother Keith. To this day, we are on The Way together. Our hearts are knit together and we share a common Hope.

But God proves his own love for us
in that while we were still sinners, Christ died for
us. Romans 5:8

Two years later, I left church in Sonora one Sunday morning to go eat Sunday brunch pancakes at Rube's Diner. This was a weekly ritual we all enjoyed—when we could afford it. I needed a ride so I climbed into a

Volkswagen Bug with a bunch of Brothers. I sat down in the front seat and there were those stickers on the dashboard. I looked at the driver, Rodney, carefully. "I know you!"

He looked at me and said, "Really? I'm not in Sonora very often. I live in Coulterville." After telling him the story of riding in his car years before, we talked all the way through brunch. Several months later, Rodney and his kids moved to Sonora. We are dearest friends to this day. I loved him then and I love him now.

HOLY GHOST

After I became a Believer, I returned to Yosemite to work. I had a summer assignment working in Tuolumne Meadows, in the high country. I knew some Christians who worked up there and I was excited to tell them that I had given my heart to Jesus. Amazingly, though, they didn't believe me. Their experience of me from the past was not very positive. It was easy to understand they'd have hesitation—a similar kind of hesitation Ananias of Damascus felt, as recorded in Acts 9:10-18, when he heard that the murderer Saul of Tarsus had converted to Christianity; although I'd imagine somewhat less extreme. They persisted in avoiding having any fellowship with me, but later that summer, a position with the Park Service collecting campground fees opened down in the Valley and I snapped it up. I was happy to return to where I had friends but none of them were Believers; they didn't know what to make of my new-found faith.

I was unfazed in believing I really had met Jesus. I had gone to a Protestant church as a kid and been to some Sunday School. My mother went to a small church in her town. Jesus was not a totally foreign name to me. Even so, I was very aware that nobody had ever told me I could meet Jesus and have a personal relationship with Him. Nobody had ever told me before that the Bible is true. This was all very new to me.

I told my mother what had happened to me. Her response was somewhat deflating at the time. "Oh yes, I had my religious experience when I was in my twenties. It's a phase which will fade with time."

"I don't think so, Mom. I don't think this is a phase. This is something profoundly real." She turned and went on eating her broccoli. I didn't really want to go to church at that time. To me, it seemed like religious ritual. I wanted this relationship, and as far as I was concerned, it was me and Jesus on the road together.

One Sunday, I put on my ranger uniform and went in to work for the 8:30 shift. My boss was a kind man named Coyt. Apologizing, he told me he'd made a mistake and I wasn't supposed to come in until 11. I went over to Degnan's, the village coffee shop, and sat in a booth with my donut. Glancing to my right, I noticed a poster labeled: Religious Services in Yosemite. There was quite a list, with an assortment of denominations. At the bottom of the list was, Non-denominational Christian. It was supposed to start at 9am. I glanced at my watch. It was now 8:50. The Yosemite Chapel was directly across the Merced River from Degnan's. I decided to check out what a non-denominational Christian church service was.

The chapel was packed, but somebody found one last folding chair for me and I sat in the very back. The minister came out and started speaking, praying, and inviting us to worship. I felt like he was talking over everyone and speaking just to me. It was riveting. The message he shared might as well have been just for my heart on that morning. Once again, I knew I was surrounded. This was not Coyt's mistake. I am supposed to be here. I'm supposed to hear these words. Jesus is speaking to me and He wants me to hear what He has to say.

When the service was over, the minister walked through the crowd right up to me, stuck out his hand and said, "Hi. My name is John. We don't get a lot of men in uniform here on Sunday. Welcome." I had never felt so welcome in all my life. He invited me to return that evening at 6pm for a Bible study. He was starting a new study in the Book of Romans. I'd never studied the Bible. That day started a whole new lifestyle for me: fellowship, worship, Bible study, hearing from God, and friends who are Believers. He's long retired now; but Pastor John is one of my dearest and most-trusted friends to this day.

I bought a new Bible. There are lots of English translations, so I bought the version that I saw John was using. I was devouring it. That summer of 1974, I never again missed a Sunday service or the two Bible studies each week. I met many wonderful Christian Brothers and Sisters; several are friends even now. But, most amazing, was what I saw in the Scriptures, many things I'd never known. But also, many things I didn't understand.

One thing which surprised me was the existence of spirits, both good and bad. I'd heard people talk of folks being "possessed by the devil," but I'd always thought that was a figure of speech. It never dawned on me there is a devil, or ghosts. One Bible study, somebody spoke up and asked John, "Pastor, isn't The Holy Spirit just a description of a feeling? Sort of like when people talk about spirit at a football game?" John, who has never been careless or excessive with words, looked at this fellow and simply replied, "The Bible calls The Holy Spirit: Him."

I mused about this when I went home. I didn't really understand anything. In my simplistic thinking I imagined that if a person could be "possessed by the devil," then certainly a person could be "possessed by The Holy Spirit." Makes sense. I started praying, "Lord, I want to be possessed by The Holy Spirit." I didn't notice anything happen. In fact, for several weeks I prayed this little prayer multiple times each day. But something *had* happened. Sometimes, I would erupt into praise and thanksgiving. Everywhere I went, all day long, I felt God was very close. Jesus was really with me. Then one evening, I felt God speaking to my heart, "You don't need to keep praying that. I have baptized you in my Holy Spirit." Later, I noticed what John the Baptist had said of Jesus:

> *I baptize you with water, but he will baptize you*
> *with the Holy Spirit.*
> Mark 1:8

At that time, I connected the dots. I realized that the Greek word translates "baptize" from the same root word which describes the process of dunking fabric in a permeating dye to color it. I had certainly tasted God's Spirit at the moment I received Jesus. But now, He permeates me. People talk about the "signs" that someone has been baptized in God's Spirit, such as speaking in tongues, or prophesying, or having some specific experience. It's clear to me that the best evidence of the fullness of God's indwelling is that His Word opens to our understanding like it never could before.

> *But the Counselor, the Holy Spirit, whom the Father*
> *will send in my name,*
> *will teach you all things and remind you of*
> *everything I have told you.*
> John 14:26

When the early disciples' leaders, Peter and John, had been put in prison, they called to God for help and prayed that they might be empowered to speak His Word with boldness, and

> *...they were all filled with the Holy Spirit*
> *and began to speak the word of God boldly.*
> Acts 4:31

I always encourage Believers to pray, just like the early disciples did and that God would fill you with His Holy Spirit!

SIN IN THE RED HOUSE

After I left Yosemite in the fall of 1974, I moved to Sonora, California. My brother, John, was still living there as part of a Christian fellowship. This group called themselves The Order of The Lamb. The unmarried members of the congregation lived in communal-style houses, separating men and women, who were mostly working, newly-converted hippies.

I moved into The Red House, which was a large, two-story red Victorian with a basement and attic, and a questionable safety status. It's still there in Sonora on Main Street, although it has since been painted other colors. It was a great old place with a huge living-room/common-room. We had Bible studies there most nights of the week, and about half the single men in The Order of the Lamb lived there. I had the bedroom at the top of the stairs, which I shared with various roommates.

Unfortunately, one of the hallmarks of the hippie movement was the notion that unbridled sexual activity was not only acceptable, but in-fact commendable for the freedom it afforded. *If it feels good, Do It!* was the cry of the hippies. For young, single adults coming from that culture, it was a huge challenge to change to a life of celibacy and purity, to wait for marriage and to pursue a monogamous life. Not everyone changed; some walked away.

The Spirit spoke to us often, and loudly, at the Red House. The fact that He spoke to us was often a deep confirmation in our souls that God was really afoot in our lives. One night, in the middle of the night, a Brother woke me up. From his room down the hall, he was awakened by The Spirit, telling him there was sin in the Red House. He came and told me, and asked me to pray. Neither of us heard anything, and the lights were all out. He went downstairs, while I prayed.

About a half hour later, he returned. He found nothing downstairs, so he continued down into the basement. There, he found a Brother on top of a pile of spare mattresses in the storage room, having sex with a girl from Sonora. She was not one of the girls from the Girls' House. Having been found out, they quickly re-dressed; the girl ran off and the Brother sat in utter surprise and embarrassment. He begged to be forgiven. Perhaps the biggest impact came when everyone realized that Our Father told us what was going on and wanted it stopped. Nobody in the Red House had any suspicions. His miracle was waking us up, moving us to action, and stopping what none of us could have possibly known was happening.

THAT GIRL

After I became a Believer, I protected myself by claiming that I was never going to get married. "It's just Jesus and me." My older brother, however, met Bonnie at *The Order of the Lamb* in Sonora and they were married on September 7, 1974. I was still working in Yosemite at that time, but I drove to Sonora for the wedding and brought my camera. John and Bonnie couldn't afford a wedding professional, so I became photographer by default. It was a gentle, charming event but the one most-poignant memory for me was at the reception. Across the room I spied the most beautiful girl I'd ever seen. We didn't meet.

Photos in 1974 were strictly film, so it was a few weeks before I could get the results. I went back to Sonora with about fifty pictures, which would be my wedding present to the nuptials. I went to the house they were renting, but after not finding them, I decided to go to the Boys' House, hoping John might be there. That didn't work, so I went to the Girls' House to hopefully find Bonnie. No luck. There were a good number of the girls there, and as I was leaving somebody said, "You're John's brother, aren't you?"

After confirming, I mentioned I had the wedding pictures for them. Immediately, the throng swarmed around me and everybody wanted to examine every picture. One of the girls said, "This is...she's the next one who's getting married." Somebody else asked me, "Are you getting married?" I squirmed a touch, amidst this group.

I gave my canned response to that question—a bold, "I don't think I'm ever going to get married." I delivered it with conviction and straight away, the voice to my immediate left said, "Me neither." I turned and gazed into the lovely green eyes of that beautiful girl I'd seen. Right then, as clear as any voice I've heard with my ears, the Voice inside said, *You're going to marry her*. I ducked out the door, pictures in hand. I didn't even know her name.

Her name is Carla.

I moved to Sonora about a month later in order to enroll in Columbia College. On Sundays, I attended the services at The Order of The Lamb. There was that girl. Everyone participated in the numerous activities of the fellowship and so I saw Carla often. Sunday services, Bible studies, Prayer meetings, pot-luck dinners...I saw her a good deal.

It didn't take very long for me to realize I was smitten and I should abandon my monastic celibacy conviction. Carla, however, had no need for me. Or any guy, for that matter. For the next several years, Carla wouldn't even so much as go out on a date with me. "I wouldn't want to create some false impression" was her standard response every time I asked her for a date. I even boldly told her one time, when my guard was down, that I mused over marrying her someday. That didn't go over well. So I prayed, and essentially gave up my fantasy. I figured I'd never get married unless I found someone I liked as much, or more, than Carla. She had set the bar.

Interestingly, despite my rationalizations, I still felt convinced that someday I would marry Carla. The fact that we had essentially no relationship didn't seem too significant to me. I was praying one time and I felt certain that The Spirit spoke to me, saying, *You'll marry her, and you'll have a son named Nathan.* I didn't share that with anybody. I tried as best I could not to think about her. I had only minor success with that. She was there at The Order of The Lamb and so was I. I saw her, across the room.

TWO BANDANAS AND TEMPTATION

In the mid-1970s, we had virtually nightly Bible Studies. Sometimes they went on late into the evening. They were often worshipful, joyful events and we left feeling blessed and often challenged.

At one point, I moved to the Gold-Rush town of Columbia, five miles north of Sonora, and lived by myself in a tiny, run-down cabin out in the sticks. It was peaceful and good for my times with Jesus but I felt less connected with the Brothers and Sisters, except for our meetings.

Late one Monday night, I got in my pickup truck after study and drove off to my cabin. I felt very upbeat about The Word. As I drove up the country road, I noticed a hitch-hiker. I pulled over and waited. I was still hippie enough to pick folks up, and there was still the perception in the mid-70s that it was relatively safe.

The door swung open and a lovely young woman jumped in. She was maybe eighteen. She was barefoot with long hair, and was wearing short cut-offs and two bandanas tied into triangles for a top. As soon as I saw her, I was rattled. I was twenty-one. I was single. I was lonely. I forced myself to look away and we drove down the road. She told me she was going to her place near Columbia and I agreed to drop her off; but otherwise I didn't say anything.

As we drove on, the girl broke the silence, asking if I knew where there was a party or something fun going on. I felt confident that the best way to squash this conversation was to say, "Well, I just came from a Bible Study at The Order of the Lamb."

She responded, "Oh, you're a Christian?"

"Yes, I am." An odd silence ensued. I certainly did all I could, restraining myself from looking at her.

After an awkward moment, she pointedly asked, "Is it true that Christians don't have pre-marital sex?" That hit me as an odd question from a stranger of the opposite sex, in the dark of the late evening. I didn't have enough composure to pray and ask God for help. I just responded, "Right. Christians who believe the Bible understand that we should wait for marriage." *That should do it*, I mused to myself.

Without missing a beat, she said, "Why? Don't you realize it feels really good?" I'm not sure what I said because I was really flying to the moon at this point. I remember she was leaning towards me and trying to make a case for why my stand was unreasonable. Thankfully, we got to her place and I was happy I'd be rid of her and be able to go home to my monastic sanctuary. But when I stopped, she didn't get out. She told me, rather insistently, that I should come in with her and that we should talk this through in more depth.

For many years as a lonely, unbelieving teen, I had dreamed of such an encounter; but it never happened. Now here I was, a young Believer, and the seeming ultimate fantasy climbs into my pickup with me and eagerly welcomes me into her little house. I was ripping into two. I didn't have a clue what to say. I certainly didn't know the Bible well enough to scripturally explain the beauty of God's pure sacrament of marriage in comparison to mere fornication.

Completely without words, I pushed myself and said, "I can't do that."

"But why?" she demanded. I like to think I'm pretty adept in an argument but right then, I could only muster, "Because God says, 'no!'" She snorted at me, jumped out and slammed the pickup door.

I drove off very shaken and got to my cabin crying. However, I can plainly say that The Spirit came and comforted me. I'd somehow done the right thing. I also realized then that I couldn't remember where her place was. That was good.

It was sometime later that I first heard the admonishment of the apostle James, where he said,

...Consider it a great joy, my brothers and sisters, whenever you experience various trials, because you know that the testing of your faith produces endurance. And let endurance have its full effect, so that you may be mature and complete, lacking nothing.
James 1:2-4

I can't claim it was joy at the time; but I rejoice now.

JAN AT THE ARONOS CLUB

When I joined in 1974, The Order of The Lamb did not have a church building. They met weekly at The Aronos Women's Research Club. "Aronos" is Sonora spelled backwards. I have no idea what they researched. But they have, to this day, a cute little meeting hall standing above the north end of Main Street. It consists of a 100-seat room with a curtained stage and kitchen off to the side. Innumerable beautiful interactions with the Almighty have happened in that hall and many of my fondest memories were born there.

I play the guitar. Before I believed in Jesus, I fantasized that I would become a rock star and because of my prowess on the guitar, beautiful girls would drape themselves upon me. It didn't happen that way. When I became a Believer, I set the guitar aside because I feared it would become a stumbling block for me. After some time, somebody found out that I could play, and that I could sing reasonably well. They recruited me to play music for the fellowship. I cut my teeth on leading worship music in The Aronos Club over many Sunday mornings and evenings. It was pretty free-form. No; actually it was borderline chaotic.

One Sunday morning, after we stopped singing praise songs, which typically went on for over an hour, I sat and Pastor Harry started his message. After some time, everyone became uncomfortably aware of a young woman standing in the back right corner of the room. She was staring with an alarmed look at the left front of the room, just to the right of the pastor. Although Harry was not easily rattled, it was unsettling for him, and he finally stopped talking and spoke to the woman and asked if she was okay.

"Jesus is standing over there." She pointed at the focal point of her staring. Harry, standing uncharacteristically still, glanced slowly to his right, then back at the woman.

"What's He doing?"

With a quivering voice, Jan—as I soon learned was her name—replied, "Nothing. He's standing there, reaching out with both of His arms. And He's looking right at me."

Harry just stood there like a statue and told her quietly, "I believe you." He then slowly continued his message, which, as I recall, lasted a long time. Maybe a half hour later, Harry again addressed Jan, "Is He still standing there?"

Jan, who was frozen in position and looking somewhat ashen, responded, "Yes. He's standing there looking at me. He's reaching out his arms."

What followed was amazing. Harry quietly told Jan to come forward because Jesus was there for her, calling her to believe and be saved. She came, and knelt, and prayed. I never knew if anyone else in the packed hall saw anything; but virtually everyone was slain. We all fell on our knees, or our faces, and many came forward with Jan. I think everyone carefully avoided going to the front left corner of the room. The meeting went far into the night. Other people gave their lives to Jesus. Many in the room were convicted of their sins and repented. We cried. We prayed. We sang and worshipped. We were filled with awe and astonished that The Lord would visit us and manifest Himself in our little country town.

Jan had been raised by Christian parents in Rocklin, a town east of Sacramento. She had never become a Believer herself, until that day. Her story, and that of her mother and father, became instrumental in leading others to Jesus. Jan grew to be a greatly loved blessing within our fellowship. I never saw, with my eyes, what Jan saw. But I know, with all my heart and from the fruit that it bore, that He was there for her, just as she saw.

THE LEAST IN THE KINGDOM

I imagine I dream like most other folks. Is there a way to know? But I've never been one to much remember what I dreamed—even right upon waking up. Frequently, I would sit with my kids at the breakfast table and they would dive into comparing their dreams. Elaborate stories with plots and intrigue and imaginative, phantasmagorical goings-on. I rarely could share in those recollections. They would say to me, "What did you dream last night, Dad?" and the best remembrance I ever came up with was, "I was laying on a hillside and watched the pelicans fly by." This dream has become a monument to me, for my kids.

But the few times God has given me a dream, it's remained vivid in my memory. Those dreams have stood out. The first one, which was humble, was nevertheless, a turning point in my life with God.

After this I will pour out my Spirit on all humanity;
then your sons and your daughters will prophesy,
your old men will have dreams, and your young
men will see visions.
Joel 2:28

I was worshiping God in our "church," the Aronos Club. We were singing. People were dancing in a circle; our

49

seating arrangement was round, with a clear area in the center for folks to dance, if they felt led to do so. It was a joyful time, with light everywhere, and hands held high in praise of Jesus. I felt very comfortable in this environment because you could *feel* the presence of God in our midst.

> *For where two or three are gathered together in my name, I am there among them.*
> Matthew 18:20

I casually glanced to my right and although I was not standing near a wall, an open door was right there. I saw a huge crowd of people on the other side of the door. They were likewise in the midst of heartfelt, joyful, active worship; but all facing forward, looking at something, or Someone, out of my view. There was a young man right near me on the other side of the door. His hands were raised in worship of nearly explosive joy. He sang and shouted; but I didn't understand him.

Finally, I got as close as I could and I asked, "What are you looking at?" I couldn't see around the corner of the door. Up to that point, he'd taken no notice of me; but my attention was fixed upon him. The young man looked at me and immediately I realized that I loved him like no person I'd ever known. I wanted to grab him and hug him; but, for reasons I didn't know, I couldn't go through the door and reach him, despite his very-close proximity. "What are you looking at?" He glanced knowingly at me, and then turned his gaze forward again. A radiant smile of joy flushed across his face. Then he turned to me again and quietly spoke. I heard him plainly, despite the din of the hall I was in, and the expanse he was in. "It's HIM!" His gaze returned to the front.

I wrenched to see what my neighbor was adoring but I couldn't see well enough to catch a glimpse. I was frustrated because I earnestly yearned to see what he saw. I didn't know what to do. So, in typical bumbling fashion I finally blurted out, "Hey! I really LOVE you!"

The praise continued on both sides of the door, unabated. But my smiling friend turned slowly to me and replied, "Me? Oh...I'm the least in the Kingdom of Heaven." I awoke in The Order of the Lamb boys' house, startled.

MY FLEECE

After two years of living in Sonora, being in fellowship in The Order of The Lamb, and living in and out of the boys' houses which the group maintained, I was settled and happy. In 1976, a group of about 120 members of our Fellowship, including Pastor Harry, felt the Spirit's call to move as a group to Salt Lake City. Our country bumpkin church would start a satellite in the urban expanse. We were flatly told that the move was not to convert Mormons. It was to preach the gospel of Jesus and lead lost souls to salvation in Him. If they happened to be Mormon, well...

Our much-loved Associate Pastor, Steve, would stay behind and shepherd the Sonora flock which included me. I had a great job as a darkroom specialist for a professional photography studio. We did mostly weddings but the owner, who was also an older, married Believer at another church in town, had talents in many styles and formats. He patiently taught me the business and I was delighted to be learning so much. It was particularly satisfying to not merely have a job; but to be learning a skill. I was not only learning from an established expert; I was learning from a Brother in Jesus.

In the unsettling division of our Fellowship into two congregations, I was asked if I would move to Utah.

I wanted none of it. I love California and I loved my job. And Carla was there: I still held onto my hope.

I owned a wonderful, restored 1954 Chevrolet step-side pickup which often was employed in helping folks who needed to haul something. A few months after the "exodus" to Utah, I was asked if I could drive my truck to Utah to haul folks' stuff. I had some days off so I agreed. Almost immediately, people started asking me if I was going to move to Utah with the rest. I flatly rejected such a notion. Their response? "Have you prayed about this?" Well, no. I hadn't; and I wasn't very interested to do so.

One of our members was forward about this matter and suggested that I ought to pray about it. Sensing my resistance, he encouraged me to get guidance from God by placing "a fleece" before Him. This referred to an old-testament action where an Israelite named Gideon received confirming direction for an unsettling matter, by employing a lamb's fleece:

> *Then Gideon said to God, 'If you will deliver Israel by my hand, as you said, I will put a wool fleece here on the threshing floor. If dew is only on the fleece, and all the ground is dry, I will know that you will deliver Israel by my strength, as you said.' And that is what happened. When he got up early in the morning, he squeezed the fleece and wrung dew out of it, filling a bowl with water. Gideon then said to God, 'Don't be angry with me; let me speak one more time. Please allow me to make one more test with the fleece. Let it remain dry, and the dew be all*

over the ground.' That night God did as Gideon requested: only the fleece was dry, and dew was all over the ground.
Judges 6: 36-40

This was not so much about a trick using a lamb's fleece as it was using an undeniable miracle to confirm what God wanted in Gideon's life. I agreed with several friends to place a fleece before God. My fleece was this: if I was in Salt Lake City and some stranger, unprovoked, offered me a job working in custom-color darkroom work, making more money than I was already making in Sonora, then I would receive that as His confirmation that I should move to Utah and join our Fellowship there. Together, we prayed and I placed my fleece to the Lord in Jesus' name.

Off I drove to Utah with a pickup full of stuff, and a friend riding along. It was summer and we were happy. I was excited to see dear friends for a visit. We stayed with friends who had already moved there and it was a heart-warming time for a couple of days.

I was going to drive back alone on Tuesday. Monday afternoon, I was walking in downtown Salt Lake past some shops, when I noticed a very-fine portrait studio. This photographer's work was clearly top tier. I stared in the window and admired the work for the quality and the style. I decided to slip in to study the photographer's technique for a few minutes. This was a typical thing for me to do when I had the chance to see other photographers' work up close.

Inside, a woman asked me if I needed some help and I stated that I liked the work and wanted to look more closely, if that was okay. She agreed that it was fine and went in back without any comment. A couple of minutes later, a burly guy walked through and noticed me admiring the photos. He stopped and chatted. We talked technique for a moment and then he admitted that he was the photographer, Andy. He asked where I was from and how I knew photography. He had never heard of Sonora, nor Gallery House, where I worked. He walked off. I looked for a minute or so longer, at which point Andy reappeared as I was leaving. He stopped me and asked, "Hey. Would you be interested in a job in my darkroom? I need another color guy and I think you have an eye for this. I could pay you..." He offered me substantially more than I made at home. I was floored.

This guy didn't even know my name. "I'm leaving for Sonora tomorrow." It didn't faze him. He encouraged me to think about it, talk to my boss, and give him a call, one way or the other. He gave me his card. "I need somebody to start next Monday." I couldn't imagine giving such short notice on the job I had. I had work waiting for me back home.

Back with my friends, I told them what happened and they all reminded me of my fleece. I felt overwhelming conviction; but I wasn't eager to move to Utah. It was a long drive home and I had a long time to ponder what had happened.

Back in Sonora, my boss told me straight out, "I knew God was going to call you to Salt Lake City. Don't worry about me. I'll find somebody to replace you. You should follow the commitment you made to God." My pastor agreed that it would dishonor God to not move after what I'd prayed and what had subsequently happened.

I stuffed all my things in a duffle bag and took the train back to Salt Lake City. I decided to sell my beautiful pickup truck to a musician friend in Sonora rather than take it with me. I realized that if I had wheels, I would likely skip town when times got tough; and I didn't trust myself. In hindsight, that was a good decision.

The following Monday, a whole new chapter opened in my life. I lived in Salt Lake City for seven years.

PART TWO

THE COMFORT I NEVER EXPECTED

On September 29, 1976, I was at an evening worship service with The Order of The Lamb in Salt Lake City. We had a pay phone in the foyer of the church, which was a frumpy store front two blocks from the temple in the center of the town. Folks were persistently getting up and going out to use the phone during the services. I'd never once used the phone there and I thought it somewhat odd that some people wanted to make their phone calls from the church. I found it stranger still that phone calls would be happening even while a service was underway.

That evening, somebody came and got me out of the service, saying, "There's a phone call for you." It was my dad. That was surprising, since we didn't communicate frequently and I hadn't talked to him since I left California. I had no idea how he discovered what the number of the church's pay phone was.

"Charlie, your mom's in the hospital. She collapsed this morning and I think you should come out to California right away. I'll pay for your ticket." I prayed with some people right then and there for my mom, and then went straight out to the Salt Lake airport. Having no luggage and wearing the clothes I had on at church, I caught a 10pm flight to Sacramento. Some Brothers from The Order of The Lamb in Sonora, Papa Bob, and Pastor Steve, were waiting for me at the airport. It was very late. They took me straight to St. Joseph's Hospital in Stockton. The hour-long drive was tense, especially since none of us really knew what to expect. We sang songs and chatted.

Once we arrived, I discovered that my dad had understated the situation. My mother had a stroke that morning and had died. Her body was being kept alive by machines, but she was gone. I wanted to believe that God would heal her and restore her. Part of me knew it wasn't going to happen. I prayed by her bedside for hours. A nurse, who was clearly a Believer, felt my broken heart and did what she could to bring some comfort. Even so, it was a bitter time. We sat in the hospital chapel, crying and praying until morning when Bob, Steve, and I headed to my brother's house in Sonora.

When we arrived, there on John's porch was Carla. She ran to the car and hugged me, silently, for a very-long time. I thought to myself, *What is* she *doing here?* I quickly got my answer, "I heard about your mom. John was down in Stockton yesterday evening. I was so worried about you." I was amazed. I didn't imagine that she'd be so concerned for me. In the wake of the hurricane which swept over me in the previous twenty-four hours, I felt a touch of peace—and also confusion.

I called my boss in Salt Lake and told him what had happened. My former boss in Sonora took me on in his shop since he had plenty of work piled up. I stayed with my friend, Rick. It was a blessing to be amongst very-trusted Brothers, both day and night. Then I decided to take a risk. After a couple of days, I asked Carla, "Would you go to hear a musical event at the College with me?" She said yes.

We went to the performance and I decided to take another risk. I put my arm gently about her shoulder. She did not shift away. After the show, she drove me the long way back to Rick's house; but we stopped along the way to talk. I can't remember what we talked about but I couldn't help myself. I kissed her. She kissed me. And again. We got to Rick's house later than expected. After Carla went home, I told him everything that had happened. Rick and I rejoiced through the night. Even now, we call that day, "The Earthquake." My life, in very short order, had taken a huge, life-changing shift.

Interestingly, the place in the Bible I had been studying right then was Genesis 24, which is the recounting of the miracle of God providing a wife, Rebekah, for Abraham's son, Isaac, subsequent to his mother Sarah's death. That day, the day of The Earthquake, the verse I had studied was:

And Isaac brought her into the tent of his mother Sarah and took Rebekah to be his wife. Isaac loved her, and he was comforted after his mother's death.
Genesis 24:67

As of this writing, Carla and I have been married for

over forty-three years. She is a great joy and comfort in my life.

SLAIN

I am not an overtly, emotional person. I doubt I fit many folk's image of a "Charismatic Christian" or a "Holy Roller." But I do seek The Spirit's fullness and His involvement in my walk, each day. I treasure His direction in my life.

Early in my new life in Salt Lake City, our fellowship, The Order of The Lamb, was asked to help with a convention at the Hotel Utah of the Full-Gospel Business Men's Fellowship International (FGBMFI.) This was a big event with hundreds of participants from around the USA. We were asked to provide support for the local arrangements. Among other things, I was helping the music team which was leading the brief times of worship associated with each session during the convention. This was a new experience for me, since I knew virtually nothing about FGBMI, and had rarely been to any Christian events, much less a conference.

The featured speaker one evening was the Founder of FGBMFI, Mr. Demos Shakarian. I had never heard him speak, but I had been told he was an articulate and colorful personality. I looked forward to hearing what he had to say. Mr. Shakarian was a very-successful American businessman of Armenian descent. He was of modest height and stature, with a humble, gentle demeanor. He had an engaging presence. His topic that evening was marriage, and the importance of purity and fidelity in the Christian walk. I don't remember virtually any of the specific content of his presentation except that he suddenly stopped abruptly and changed what he had been speaking about. He looked out upon the seated crowd before him with love and conviction. "I feel The Spirit wants all of the married men who are here to stand right now. I want to pray for you."

A large percentage of the crowd stood. Slowly, but steadily, a groundswell of spontaneous worship grew as he prayed for us. He asked us to come forward, or step into the aisles, so that we could form groups of five to ten men and we could pray directly for each other. I was near the front and next to an aisle. I went forward, found a group of men, and joined in the prayer. It felt wonderful, loving, perfect.

There is no objective manner for describing the feeling of closeness and sheer presence which I felt, as everybody surely did, of God's Holy Spirit that evening as we were praying. It was pure and true. Nobody was going to leave, and nobody wanted it to end. Some men prayed aloud, and some silently. But the atmosphere was reverent, holy and loving. Our unexpected, spontaneous time of prayer and worship continued on for some time.

I felt a tap on my shoulder. Turning, I saw Mr. Demos Shakarian himself staring me straight in the eyes. Even now, I remember the sense of love and humble compassion as he asked me, "May I pray for you?" Being newly married, I wasn't going to reject his prayers.

"Sure!" With a beaming smile, which I can see as I write this, he raised his hands toward me and prayed. He didn't touch me. Suddenly, he interjected, with confidence and conviction, "Be filled with the Holy Ghost!" Immediately, and quite unexpectedly, I floated over backwards with a feeling of overwhelming joy and fell to the ground, face up. I'm sure somebody caught me, but I have no idea who. I staggered to my feet with a feeling of elation. I had no idea what had just happened. There he stood, staring at me as though he could see into me, with eyes of love and joy.

With a beaming smile on his face, he quietly asked, "Isn't Jesus wonderful?" I don't know if I said anything or just nodded. Immediately, Mr. Shakarian again raised his hands towards me, and with a tone of triumph repeated, "Be filled with The Holy Ghost!" I could do nothing except, once again, float to the floor over backwards. I picked myself up, found his eyes still fixed on mine and for a third time, with hands raised towards me he commanded, "Be filled with The Holy Ghost!" In a dream-like manner, I wafted backwards and found myself staring up, and thinking, "What is happening?"

This time when I stood, I saw Mr. Shakarian smiling at me and turning away to pray for somebody else. It was a happy, knowing smile. He gently wagged his head and gave a soft, benevolent chuckle as he walked away. As for me, I was completely filled with joy and confidence in God. It was a sensation as though nothing else was happening in the universe at that moment. I turned around towards the group of men I'd been praying with. Among them at this point was a friend from our home church, Kenny, who was beaming at me with approval.

"Isn't that amazing?" he chimed. "I don't even believe in this sort of thing, and when I saw him pray for somebody else, and that person's response was identical to yours, I thought to myself, 'Well, he's not going to do that to me!' But, in fact, he walked over to me and DID pray for me, and the very same thing happened to me. I don't know what happened."

Even now, I'm not sure I know what happened. What I do know, however, is that event opened a new move of The Spirit in my life for some time to come. The sense of God's immediate presence with me was heightened. The Word seemed opened up to me. I could feel Him working in my life to transform me. God wasn't "out there." He was "right here." He is with me; He is in me; He is working through me.

I never saw or heard Demos Shakarian again. And I didn't join FGBMFI, although I did attend a few local meetings or breakfasts they hosted in subsequent years. But God, meeting me there, can't be forgotten.

DID JESUS REALLY DIE AND
FORGIVE ALL OUR SINS?

I know that at the most-basic level, a "miracle" is where God in the supernatural, interacts with this natural world. That can be subtle, and that can be highly dramatic. But the result is the same: it changes people. If we consider that Believers in Jesus have been given the gift of the Holy Spirit, which is a miracle in itself, then there are interactions with God all the time. There are miracles everywhere. Sadly, we as Believers, sometimes lose sight of the fact that this is not the normal experience of those who do not know Jesus. And Believers can become so accustomed to God interacting with them personally, that they lose sight of the fact that it is God who is at work.

Sometimes the miracle is something said which changes a life for good. Consider the apostle Peter. He was, for the most part, a pretty outspoken, self-confident man. At the Last Supper, the day before Jesus was crucified, Jesus told his twelve disciples that they would all abandon Him. To this, Peter boldly responded:

> *"Lord," (Peter) told him, "I'm ready to go with you both to prison and to death." "I tell you, Peter," (Jesus) said, "the rooster will not crow today until you deny three times that you know me."*

Luke 22:33-34

Jesus didn't accept this façade of bold confidence. It wasn't but a few hours later, that night:

> *They lit a fire in the middle of the (high priest's) courtyard and sat down together, and Peter sat among them. When a servant saw him sitting in the light, and looked closely at him, she said, "This man was with him too." But he denied it: "Woman, I don't know him." After a little while, someone else saw him and said, "You're one of them too." "Man, I am not!" Peter said. About an hour later, another kept insisting, "This man was certainly with him, since he's also a Galilean." But Peter said, "Man, I don't know what you're talking about!" Immediately, while he was still speaking, a rooster crowed. Then the Lord turned and looked at Peter. So Peter remembered the word of the Lord, how he had said to him, "Before the rooster crows today, you will deny me three times." And he went outside and wept bitterly.*

Luke 22:55-62

A plain sentence from Jesus, and later, a look in the eye was enough to cause the miracle of a life changed forever. This was the same apostle Peter who later wrote:

> *Humble yourselves, therefore, under the mighty hand of God, so that he may exalt you at the proper time, casting all your cares on him, because he cares about you.*

1 Peter 5:6-7

In 1980, Carla and I went to a marriage conference which was being promoted by the church. It was especially exciting to us because we were expecting our first child, and we were around 3-4 months into the pregnancy. We were elated. While at the conference, much to our horror, Carla started feeling contractions. I took her to the hospital. After an all-night struggle, full of prayers and hopes, she miscarried. It was devastating. I was not only sad; I was mad.

Carla stayed at the hospital getting some sleep, and I went home for a short time, wallowing in my anger. It was Sunday morning and I did not go to church. While I was home, my dear friend, David, showed up at the house. He said nothing; but it was evident he knew what had happened. I'm not sure how he knew. I did not want to talk with him. I walked into another room without a word. He followed me. I walked into a different room. He followed there, as well. After some silent cat-and-mouse evasion, I ended up in my bedroom, and he followed. I sat on the corner of the bed, and he sat next to me. Not a word. I was angry.

David, of all people, is one person who understands the issue here. He has lost four of his children. But he remains faithful. He does not shake his fist at God.

Finally, sitting on the corner of the bed, David spoke. "I'll tell you what you're thinking. 'What did I do wrong?' Or maybe it's, 'What didn't I do?' Let me say this: what you're really asking in posing those questions is, 'Did Jesus really die on the cross and forgive all of my sins?' That's the question. You need to settle in yourself the answer."

I turned and glared at David. He said no more. He went home, and I went back to the hospital. I couldn't shake my fist at God after that. It was a miracle.

Truly I tell you, anyone who hears my word and believes him who sent me has eternal life and will not come under judgment but has passed from death to life.
John 5:24

I SAW JESUS!

There is no doubt that Jesus was far more interested in the purity of a person's heart than their religious practices. In his first major oration, the Sermon on the Mount, he commenced with his emphasis on how we are to know God, and be known by God, and not merely know about God. In his final prayer on record, He spoke to His Father:

> *This is eternal life: that they may know you, the only true God, and the one you have sent — Jesus Christ.*
> John 17:3

It's a two-way street. He wants to know us as well; but it only happens when we initiate a life with Him. We correctly state, when we are born again as Believers, that we have initiated our relationship with Jesus. Mere religious practice clearly doesn't meet His standards, and he didn't mince words with the Pharisees about that:

> *On that day many will say to me, 'Lord, Lord, didn't we prophesy in your name, drive out demons in your name, and do many miracles in your name?' Then I will announce to them, 'I never knew you. Depart from me, you lawbreakers!'*
> Matthew 7:22-23

I was taught that a good way to get to know Him is to read the four gospels, again and again, and see yourself as a person in the crowd following Him. Meditate on the things he says. And He gets to know us as we bring all matters to Him in our prayers.

Don't worry about anything, but in everything, through prayer and petition with thanksgiving, present your requests to God. And the peace of God, which surpasses all understanding, will guard your hearts and minds in Christ Jesus.
Philippians 4:6-7

Casting all your cares on him, because he cares about you.
1 Peter 5:7

Early on in my walk with Jesus, I realized that "I know Him." If He walked into the room, I'd recognize Him immediately. His Word shows us how He thinks; how He feels; what He wants. And I started to see that He is always coming after me. He knows me, too.

I have always enjoyed riding my bicycle. There was even a time when I joined a local bike club and raced regularly with them; although having kids put an end to that—it takes too much time. One day, in Salt Lake City, a friend and I went riding and he asked me, "Where's your helmet?" I didn't own one. My friend quipped, "They have a name for your behavior. It's called 'suicidal.'" After some grumbling, I went to Fisher's Bike Shop, a few blocks from our house, and ordered one. They didn't stock them then; helmets were a new phenomenon in 1980.

Then came September 20, 1980. At the time, I was working for an engineering team near the University of Utah, where I'd recently received a BS in Electrical Engineering. It was 5:30 and I jumped on my bike and started racing home. About halfway there, riding down a steep hill, I approached an intersection with a green light. I was going for it. Just as I entered the intersection, an oncoming car, without warning or signaling, turned left immediately in front of me. I didn't have time to touch my brakes, or even say something rude. I smashed into the side of the car and flew right over the top of it. I landed on my head and my right shoulder. The driver of the car told the police she'd never even seen me. I barely remember the accident, or the impact, or the pain. I laid unconscious, bleeding in the intersection.

The reason I was hurrying was I'd just received a call from Fisher's Bike Shop, which closes at 6pm. My bike helmet was ready for me to pick up.

The first memory I have after the accident, was the jolt of the gurney as they raised me off the ground to shove me into the ambulance. It seemed like there were people everywhere, swirling all about me. I couldn't remember the accident. I could remember nothing. Literally. I didn't know who I was, where I was, or what had happened. On the drive to Holy Cross Hospital, which was where Carla worked, I asked the paramedic, "Where are you taking me?"

"To the hospital emergency room."

"What happened?"

"You were in an accident."

"Am I going to die?"

"We think you'll be all right."

I looked away for a second, then looked back at him. I asked the paramedic, "Where are you taking me?"

"To the hospital emergency room."

"What happened?"

"You were in an accident."

"Am I going to die?"

"We think you'll be all right."

This repetitive conversation occurred some number of times and I'm pretty sure the paramedic was happier once they dropped me off at the ER. By then, I'd lapsed again into unconsciousness and had no awareness of the ambulance or the hospital staff.

What I was aware of was that Jesus came and spoke to me. I couldn't say what He looked like, nor can I recall our surroundings. I know we spoke for some time; but I remember only a scant part of the conversation. Interestingly, I knew Him immediately, and felt very comfortable, and even overjoyed, to be with Him. It was sublimely peaceful.

I regained consciousness in the emergency room, amidst a huge swirl of doctors and nurses, and needles and stuff. I had no idea where I was. My conversation with the doctor picked up right where I'd left off with the paramedic.

"What happened?"

This person, however, had a different approach. "Do you know who you are?"

"No."

"Do you remember where you live?"

"No."

"Do you know what time it is?"

"No."

"What did you have for breakfast?"

"Um, grapefruit? No, cereal? No...I don't know!" Glancing to the other side, I asked the nurse who was poking me with a needle, "What happened?" And then I volunteered, "I saw Jesus! We sat and talked! Isn't that wonderful?!"

"Uh huh."

Evidently, this pair of conversations repeated for some time until the doctor tapped me lightly on my undamaged shoulder. Turning, I saw Carla, looking like an angel, standing next to me. She was concerned.

"Do you know who this person is?"

I looked long and hard at her. "No. But I think she's my best friend!" That brought a smile to her face. "Yes, I think you're right."

Immediately, I blurted out to Carla, "I saw Jesus! We talked! Do you know what He said?"

She, with some excitement, replied, "No. Tell me."

"He told me, 'All of your sins are forgiven.' Isn't that wonderful?"

She was crying, "That's...that's wonderful!"

I turned to the nurse, "Isn't that wonderful?"

"Uh huh."

I turned to the tech standing there, "Isn't that wonderful?"

"Yeah."

I swung about and asked the wide-eyed doctor, "Isn't that wonderful?"

With some jitter to his voice, he replied, "Uh, yeah. That's just wonderful."

Eventually, they let Carla take me home. I was quite groggy, and they told her to wake me up every hour and talk to me. I recognized nothing; but I would get up and walk about.

"We live here?" This query cycled again and again. She had to keep her eye on me any time I was awake. If she didn't, I'd just wander: into the back yard, into the street, up into the hills.

I had full amnesia for at least a week. I spent almost all my waking time staring at things and listening to Christian music on records. It was wonderfully comforting, and I felt safe and joyful. I didn't know anybody, including Carla, and I couldn't focus my attention on anything for more than a few seconds.

Jesus was there, very close, the entire time. I could feel myself coming back very slowly, but I frankly didn't want to. It was so wonderful to be so close to Jesus.

At the doctors' advice, Carla had a host of folks who knew me with me all day long while she went to work. This was partly to jar my memory back; but also to keep me from getting up and wandering away without any clue where I was, or where I was going. Most of these folks were from our fellowship, Calvary Chapel of Salt Lake City; but some were from work; some were family.

My friend, Brad, came over and played chess with me. I'd played many games with him over the years; but had never beaten him; until now. "Hey! It's your move. Are you going to play, or stare out the window?" I'd glance down at the board, having forgotten I was playing. I'd quickly make a move and go on daydreaming. We played like this for hours, and he never beat me, even once. Brad was very annoyed at me over this. I couldn't even remember his name; how could I beat him at chess?

My friend, David, came over. "Hey. You're going with me on a field trip to the sporting-goods store." I hadn't been out at all. While we were there, he sat me down and said, "Stay here while I try these clothes on." A few minutes later, he came back; but I was nowhere to be found. David went into a panic trying to find me. *Carla's going to kill me! How could I lose him like this?* Actually, I don't know where he found me; but thankfully it was before I got run over by a truck in the street.

My boss, Kent, came over. He brought the whole team I worked with. They all were smiling, friendly, chatty. I had no idea who any of them were. Carla told me, "This is Kent, your boss." I didn't know I had a boss.

"Don't I have to have a job to have a boss?"

She looked a little annoyed, "Oh you have a job. A really good one. You're an engineer!"

That one got me. "An engineer? Don't you have to go to college to become an engineer?" Everyone fidgeted and looked at Carla, who was clearly distressed. All those years she had supported me while I was at the University of Utah. Down the drain?

It took quite a while; but memories started to return. At the same time, the joy and intimacy of the immediate presence of Jesus slowly wafted away. What remains? "All your sins are forgiven."

A man that hath friends must show himself friendly: and there is a friend that sticketh closer than a brother.
Proverbs 18:24 (KJV)

HAVING OUR FIRST SON

Despite my strange, youthful notions that I'd never marry, I had a deep sense I'd marry Carla someday. From the moment I first saw her, and even before she would have anything to do with me. I also felt like God had shown me that our first kid would be a boy, and we'd name him Nathan. Nathan: "The Gift of God." I never shared this with anybody; certainly not Carla. I was afraid that talking about such a thing would sound presumptuous, and even borderline arrogant.

Every time Carla became pregnant, we jokingly named each of our unborn children with a pet name: Bud, Oscar, Petunia, etc. But as The Day approached, we always talked a great deal about names for our kids. By the due date, we had picked a boy's name and a girl's name. The moment we knew their gender—this was in the days before they had reliable pre-natal tests for ascertaining this—they had a name.

With our firstborn, this process was long and drawn out. We both had a leaning towards family names; but not exclusively. The girl's name came first; but right up to the birth, we hadn't settled on the boy's. Maybe out of pride; maybe out of fear; I'm not sure; but I never whispered the name, Nathan. The day before Friday,

August 14, 1981, his birth day, somebody in passing said the name.

Carla spoke up, "What about Nathan? What do you think of that name?"

I blurted out, "Yes! The Gift of God." She looked at me somewhat surprised, seeing I knew what the name meant without consulting the baby-name book. It was settled. He is The Gift of God.

THE GUYS WITH THE GIMPY LEGS

I learned about High-Sierra backpacking in the Boy Scouts, and I've loved the mountains, hiking, and camping ever since. A long dream of mine had been to do a "cross country" hike from East to West across the Sierra Nevada mountains. Years before I ever did the hike, I mapped out the route: leave out of Independence, California (on highway US-395, the North-South two-lane highway which parallels the Sierras), climb up over Echo Coll, which straddles the Sierra Crest, and go west through Evolution Basin in King's Canyon National Park, descending until reaching Courtwright Reservoir's dam. It's a fantastic, seventy-mile trek through vast stretches of wilderness.

In fall 1981, the opportunity arose to do the trek with my experienced hiking buddy and good friend, Orville ("Orv.") He had been the Best Man at my wedding, and his wife, Carol, is one of Carla's best friends. At the time, we lived in Salt Lake City, and Orv and Carol lived in Bass Lake, on the west side of the Sierras. Both Carla and Carol had little kids by then, and they were delighted to spend a week hanging out with each other, while Orv and I did the long-desired hike. The plan was the Girls would drop us off in Independence, and then pick us up far to the west at Courtwright dam in seven days. We kissed and parted company, as Orv and I started our epic journey.

Orv and I had worked together in Yosemite for almost three years. When we first met, neither of us was a Believer. And when I met Jesus in Oregon, I returned a particularly changed person. It struck Orv quite by surprise. He didn't imagine I was the type to become a "Jesus Freak." It wasn't more than a few months, though, before he followed into The Way with me. He joined in with John's Bible study in Romans at Yosemite Chapel. We were baptized by John in the Merced River together in August, 1974. Although our careers took us separate ways, we've remained tightest friends. This hike together was a long-anticipated adventure.

The dream of leisurely hiking, fishing and camping took a twist on the first day. Having spent the first half of the day doing the grueling climb up to the summit of Echo Coll, we commenced to descend on the West side and very soon, I fell and seriously hurt my right knee. If we'd had a bit more sense and a bit less pride, we would have turned around then and gone back to Independence. But feigning that I was "ok" and would pull through, we proceeded west. It didn't take long before we both knew I was really hurt. We continued, slowly. By the third day, we realized we'd have no time for layover days to fish and explore. We would be lucky to make Courtwright in seven days, hiking from dawn to dusk. And that included having Orv carry a good deal of the supplies which had been in my pack.

On the fourth day, things got substantially worse. We were hiking west out of Evolution Valley, and then Orv fell and he, in like manner to me, hurt his right knee, seriously. We could only proceed west, at that point. In all likelihood, we were a ridiculous sight, hobbling along. Our hike was misery, instead of joy.

By the time we got to day seven, we were clearly nowhere near Courtwright Reservoir. It would yet be a full day before we'd reach our destination, and only after some extremely painful hiking. Both Orville and I had worked for the Park Service in Yosemite, and we knew that the Rangers send Search and Rescue teams after missing hikers. They also make the hikers pay for the costs to perform the Search, after they're found. We were worried. We also worried about the Girls and how they might panic, having driven up to the rendezvous point (about a ninety-minute drive from Bass Lake) to find we weren't there. Orv and I decided to pray for guidance. We received a calm in our hearts and concluded that we should press on, trusting that things would work out.

After about twenty-four hours, we trudged onto the dam of Courtwright Reservoir. Minutes later, the car came around the bend and the Girls sprung out to greet us and to hear our dismal story. Orv and I were both startled not only to see them right then; but to see them so calm and joyful. Carol quickly informed us: they had arrived the day before; but obviously found nothing. After waiting about an hour, they prayed, and both felt a calm assurance that we were okay, and that they should go back to Bass Lake. They would return the next day. So upon seeing us, they were elated to find us, exactly as they had anticipated after praying the previous day.

Carla and I went back to Salt Lake City, and Orville and Carol returned to work in Bass Lake. But the near-term news was not good. Both Orv and I went to our doctors to find out what was wrong. Both of us, evidently, had torn a ligament in our respective right knees. We iced our wounds, wrapped the knees, and hoped against hope that things would improve. That was not what happened. For both of us, our knees got worse. It was now closing in on Thanksgiving, and we both were told, independently, that we would have to undergo surgery to fix our damaged knees. I didn't have insurance, nor the time (I was in graduate school at the University of Utah), and this was not good news at all.

At that time, Carla and I were part of Calvary Chapel of Salt Lake City. I was a Board Member, and I taught a weekly "New Christians" Bible study each Monday. We had about twenty-five participants, all of whom had recently become Believers in Jesus. I loved teaching "Christianity 101," and I loved my Group. That mid-November week was cold and snowing, and our study group arrived at 7pm at a home in town, taking off our layers and gathering together for the week's lesson. But sitting down, I couldn't think about teaching. All I could think about was my throbbing knee, and the fact that the next day I was supposed to show up for a "pre-op" visit in anticipation of my surgery. I was not happy, and I couldn't concentrate at all.

In frustration, I didn't even start the study. "I'm sorry, folks, but I can't even imagine giving the study tonight: my knee hurts so bad. All I can think about is the pain." Everybody stood up, got their layers back on, and headed for the door and the cold outside. Right at the door, a twenty-year-old man, named Blain, who worked at the local grocery store as a stock boy, and had only been a Christian for a month or two, spoke up. He was a very gentle, quiet soul who rarely spoke. "Um, Charlie. You were telling us in an earlier study that we ought to pray for everything. Shouldn't we pray for you?" My response was not very gracious: "You want to pray for me? Fine. Do it." They all crowded around me at the front door, laying hands on me and waiting in silence. Finally, somebody spoke up, "Well, Blain, aren't you going to lead a prayer?" I don't think he'd ever done such a thing. After a few moments of nervous shuffling, out came Blain's prayer: "Uh, God? We really like Charlie. Make him better. Amen." I liked his humble attempt. I thanked him, and we headed for the door.

Then I noticed on my first step that my knee didn't hurt anymore. At all. I stopped cold and said, "Hey folks! Wait a minute." I poked my knee a bit. No pain. I started jumping up and down on my right leg. No pain. "I think God just healed my knee!" Everyone was startled and dumbfounded. Turning back into the house, off came the jackets and sweaters once again. We had a great Bible study that evening.

I cancelled the doctor visit for Tuesday, and pondered all day what had happened. For me, this had special significance because I had been wrestling with the concept of effectual prayer. Questions like, "How should I pray?" Who can be heard? How faithful is faithful enough? And many other questions. The timing on this was not arbitrary: I had just met with a Brother a few days earlier who had fallen into the trap of believing that if we really believe God, He will always answer every prayer we make, and exactly as we ask. I knew in my heart that this concept was not correct; but this particular Brother was older than I am and had been a Believer far longer than I had. He had, over the years, earned my respect, and so his insistence this "new teaching he'd been learning," although not compelling, was hard to dispute. I had been asking God what He thought about this "new teaching" and what I should learn.

In one swift action, I got the message: it's all His work, and His will. His answer to my prayers has nothing to do with how good I've been, or how fancy my prayer is, or how confident I am. Healing my knee, God had knocked down so many false notions which some of my well-meaning, but ill-informed, friends and Christian teachers had taught me.

Late that Tuesday afternoon, I called my friend Orville and told him what had happened the night before. I knew he also was scheduled to have surgery pretty soon. There was an eerie silence on the phone; although I knew he was listening carefully. Finally, Orv said, "What time did this happen?" "About 7:30pm." Salt Lake City is one hour ahead of the Pacific Time zone where he lived. After a pause, my friend spoke up, "Well. At 6:30pm yesterday, the pain in my right knee vanished. It has not come back."

Neither of us ever had surgery or even went back to our doctors about this. Neither of us has had knee problems since.

MICHAELINO'S ITALIAN RESTAURANT

I was a founding member of Calvary Chapel of Salt Lake City. The national outreach called Shiloh Youth Revivals had a ministry house in Salt Lake. In fact, it was the Shiloh House in Eugene Oregon where I had given my life to Jesus; but I didn't know any of the Shiloh folks in Salt Lake, until the organization, as whole, decided to disband in 1978. They had around 55 houses all over the USA, and most, if not all, were basically abandoned to fend for themselves. The Salt Lake group (about a dozen people) decided to keep meeting, and they needed a worship leader. I was involved in leading worship music at The Order of the Lamb, and some of the Shiloh folks asked if I'd come over to the Shiloh house on Sunday afternoons and lead worship with them. Although it raised some eyebrows, both with my wife as well as some of my friends at The Order of the Lamb, I agreed to help out.

Very quickly, one of the national leaders of Shiloh, David Stewart, felt that God wanted him to move to Salt Lake City and become the Pastor of the remnant of Believers who had been part of the Shiloh house there, under the banner of Calvary Chapel of Salt Lake City. I loved David from the moment I met him, and quickly saw that he was gifted and was an exceptional teacher of God's Word. It was affirmed that he was called to Salt Lake City by the fact that the fellowship experienced amazing growth over the subsequent five years, while David was the Pastor. The Salt Lake fellowship also planted seven other Calvary Chapel fellowships during that time, all of which remain as of this writing. After David came, I departed from The Order of the Lamb and became part of Calvary Chapel of Salt Lake City, full time. Spiritually, for me, it was time to move on; although the previous years had been marvelous.

After Calvary Chapel became a stable fellowship, David Stewart decided we should have a "Board," which would be administratively overseers for the church. I was asked to be a Board member. Prior to agreeing to that proposition, Carla and I met with David to discuss what the duties would be, and what would be expected of us. Most of what we were told was somewhat expected; but one thing surprised us: David asked us to not drink alcohol, at all, while I served on the Board.

Neither Carla nor I are "big drinkers," but we did find it surprising to be asked to re-enter the age of Prohibition. Carla took it a step further, telling David, "I'm not sure how I feel about committing to something which, in my mind, seems 'legalistic' in nature." David was firm on this point because of the predominantly Mormon environment we were living in. Although Mormons were not perceived as a specific target with whom we ought to share the gospel with, any more than other folk, we certainly shared God's

Word with them, as the opportunity arose. And they did have certain religious customs which they held to, notably, not drinking alcohol.

David asked Carla and me, "Don't you have acquaintances at work, or school or elsewhere, who are Mormon, and they would reject your Christian testimony if they knew you drink? Can you think of one?"

After some thought, Carla said, "Well, there is Dr. Middleton at work. He's a Mormon Bishop, and I've been sharing the gospel with him. I think he likes me and respects me. I wouldn't want to have a drink around him: it would surely create a stumbling block for him, and probably negate my testimony in his mind."

David was immediate in his response: "Well, for Dr. Middleton's sake, would you be willing to commit to a no-alcohol policy while Charlie serves on the Board?" After Carla and I talked it over between ourselves, we agreed to David's proposition. I served on Calvary Chapel's Board, and we abstained. It wasn't really a big deal for us, given the perspective David had shared.

A few years later, I was asked to fly to Oregon for a day on a work-related matter. I got back to Salt Lake fairly late, and Carla picked me up at the airport. Driving home, she pointed out that there hadn't been enough time to fix dinner, so we decided to go to Michaelino's Italian Restaurant, a few blocks from our house because they had later hours than other places. They seated us way in the back; actually, in a very remote, romantic spot. It was darker because our table was adjacent to their big banqueting table, which was vacant, seeing it was a late on a week night. The server came up and took our order.

She asked, "Would you like a glass of red wine to go with your dinner?" It was late; we were tired; things were romantic and secluded; our house was only a couple blocks away. Why not?

We looked at each other, struggling with our commitment. Finally, the decision poured out, "We decided to abstain, and so we should stick with it." We thanked the server, and ordered something else to drink with our lasagna.

A few minutes later, while we were eating, the lights came up and people started coming in to sit at the banquet table. Within about five minutes, the adjacent, large table was almost full and in walked the guest of honor. It was Dr. Middleton. Before he sat, he noticed Carla and immediately came over to say hello. It was a one-evening family reunion celebration; but he was delighted to interrupt his occasion to acknowledge Carla, who had earned his admiration at work. He introduced her to his wife and some others. When they sat at their table, Carla turned to me with a look of shock on her face that I'll never forget. Although we didn't talk about it until we got home, we couldn't stop thinking of David Stewart's words from several years earlier.

SHINING THE LIGHT OR CASTING OUT DARKNESS

Calvary Chapel of Salt Lake City started as a very-low budget fellowship. Essentially, our one expense was paying our pastor, David Stewart. I'm embarrassed that we didn't pay him anywhere near as much as we should have. We didn't have a building; instead, we met at the Senior Citizens' Center, just east of downtown, every Sunday. It cost $25 a week, for a few hours in their multi-purpose room. Humble though it was, this was a very special time. We grew exponentially, and mostly from unchurched newcomers and new Believers. Very few came from other, existing churches. There were, like myself, some exceptions, though.

One person, Ben, had come from a Baptist church. He was a big man, with long hair and a distinctive presence. He played music well, and was quite articulate. He had been a Believer for years, and had a good knowledge of Scripture. He almost immediately initiated a small-group Bible study in his house south of the City, and a fair number of people participated. In general, the Board at Calvary Chapel encouraged such "kinship groups" in order to allow our membership to explore faith in Jesus at a deeper level than might otherwise be possible for those who only had fellowship on Sunday mornings.

I got to know Ben through Sunday meetings and our music ministry; but I didn't go to his study, simply because I also led a study in our part of town, and I felt committed to those who fellowshipped with us. Over time, though, I heard from people on Sundays about Ben's study. According to those folks, who had attended his group to some level, his standard practice was each week to review what our Pastor, David Stewart, had taught that previous Sunday and then to "correct" what had been taught. Evidently, Ben fancied himself to be a Bible scholar, and he didn't have as high a regard for David's understanding, as for his own. I would have dismissed what I'd heard as a rumor, or gossip, except over time I got the same message from multiple sources.

I found this situation to be quite odd for two reasons. First, Ben faithfully came each Sunday to Calvary Chapel, and appeared to be quite engaged. I'd never heard him plant seeds of dissent. Secondly, I found David's teaching to be powerful and overwhelmingly sound. Furthermore, I saw enormous good fruit coming from the Sunday teaching, and I had a hard time imagining how Ben might find fault with it.

After some months of this going on, I decided to discuss the situation with David and suggest that he confront Ben about being an agent of discord in our budding fellowship. I don't know if David had already heard about Ben's behavior; but he certainly didn't react strongly to hearing of it.

To my surprise, our pastor simply said, "Thank you for telling me. We should pray for Ben. I'm not going to confront him. It's not possible to cast out darkness. I will continue, as best I can, to shine the Light into the darkness, and that Light will take care of any problem." David never did confront Ben; and neither did I. However, I did continue to feel somewhat wary of Ben after that, and had little to do with him.

The revelation of your words brings light and gives understanding to the inexperienced.
Psalms 119:130

Over two years later, I saw God act. We had a Tuesday-night prayer meeting, held at a Believer's home right in the middle to town. I virtually always went to the prayer meeting, and so did David Stewart. It was often a quiet, reverent event where we prayed for anything which came to the attention of anyone who attended. For me, this was always an important weekly event. One week, not long before I moved from Salt Lake City, I was at the prayer meeting, as was David. I also noticed Ben was there, although he was infrequent in attending the prayer meeting. As the evening progressed, at one point it was clear to all that Ben was sobbing. His crying grew to the point where folks gathered around him and started praying for him.

Eventually, he suddenly blurted out, "I'm sorry! I need for you all to forgive me! I have been secretly contradicting what David has been teaching in our church, and I've been a source of division in doing so. Just now, I feel that the Holy Spirit showed me how wrong I've been and He has commanded me to repent.

I feel terrible. I need all of you, including David, to forgive me. I need to change!"

I can't think of many times where I've experienced such a dramatic, sincere repentance by a Brother. The atmosphere at the prayer meeting was wonderful, and we all prayed and cried with Ben. I talked with him later about what had happened. Nobody had ever talked to him about what he'd been doing; but the guilt inside had been growing: he knew as time went on that what he was engaged in was wrong, and he couldn't figure out how to get free of his sin until that prayer meeting. David never said anything to me about what happened.

A month or two later, I moved away. But I heard from my friends who stayed in Salt Lake City that Ben grew in faith, and became an important leader in the fellowship. I also heard recently, now years later, that Ben eventually moved to Southern California and became a pastor of a Calvary Chapel fellowship there.

TIME TO LEAVE: IT'S IN HIS HANDS

In the fall of 1982, I was working for an engineering group based at the University of Utah doing VLSI Design (Very Large Scale Integrated-Circuitry.) Life was good: I had two baby boys, Nathan and Edward; my wife, Carla, was happy; we loved our church, Calvary Chapel of Salt Lake City; I was in graduate school, part-time, working towards a Master of Science in Electrical Engineering. I had a great job, with a great boss and co-workers, making good money; we had a fine house, on the hill above the valley. God was moving in our lives. Family and good friends surrounded us.

Mid-November—quite unexpectedly—my boss, Kent, came to my office to tell me that the contract which paid for our work was changing in about six months. I was taken by surprise because all of the feedback I'd received about our work had been positive. The results we were getting were eagerly being adopted by the industry. Kent told me if I wanted to continue to work with the group, my job description had to dramatically change, and the change was in a technical direction I distinctly did not want to go. I was very disturbed by this news.

Only a few days later, I had my monthly, scheduled lunch meeting with David Stewart, our pastor. I was on the Board at Calvary Chapel and David met with each Board member, one-monthly. At lunch, I told him that I might have to find a new job, and I would like his prayers, joining with Carla and me, that we would know God's leading in this matter. I also conveyed how disturbed I was about this change.

David looked up from his hamburger with some amazement and immediately replied, "The Lord showed me the other day that this would happen. I was praying for you, and He told me what He was going to do." The intrigue was unbearable and I wanted to know what was in store. To my surprise, David followed up by saying, "He also told me I should not tell you what He showed me; but that you would come back to me and confirm what He had told me." This was not the response I wanted. I went away from lunch somewhat discouraged. I almost felt like David was toying with me; and to me this was a very-serious matter.

Because six months is a good stretch of time, I did not aggressively pursue finding a new job. I kept doing what I was doing, and hoped I'd just wake up from this bad dream. A few weeks later, I was scheduled to go to a big engineering conference in San Francisco. One of our research collaborators, a professor from Cornell University, Jeff Frey, called me before the conference and asked if I was going. He asked if he'd see me there. Upon hearing I was also attending the San Francisco event, he mentioned that he could make his connecting flight in Salt Lake City, and he'd like to take an extra day to come up and visit our lab, if that was okay with our team. I loved the attention, and I'd never met Prof. Frey in person. I felt honored by his proposal. I said I'd pick him up at the Salt Lake airport the day before the conference started.

In one of the most stunning encounters I've ever experienced, I walked up to Prof. Frey at the Salt Lake City International Airport, shook his hand, and his first words were, "I want you to quit your job here, come join my group at Cornell, and work on a brand new project I'm starting there. You can earn your Ph.D. working with me."

As we drove to the University, it was clear Prof. Frey had little interest in the VLSI Lab. He was there to recruit me. He described the project and it was dead-center in my interest area, and exactly the research I wanted to work on. I pointed out that I hadn't applied to Cornell's Ph.D. Program. "Well, then do." I pointed out that I had a family with kids, and we'd not be able to make it on a graduate-student stipend.

"How much would you have to make?" I needed to talk it over with Carla and get back with him on that. He went on his way to San Francisco and I joined him the next day. In the interim, Carla and I had a pretty wild night discussing this unbelievable, and totally-unexpected new opportunity which literally dropped out of the sky upon us. And, at such a time.

In San Francisco, I told Prof. Frey I was interested but I wouldn't take action to quit my job, nor come to Ithaca, New York, unless I got accepted to Cornell University's Ph.D. Program and unless he could assure me of getting $16,000 a year as a student stipend while I worked on the Project. That amount of money was about twice the normal stipend amount and Prof. Frey recoiled at my condition. Even so, he encouraged me to apply to Cornell, and he would see if the research sponsor would pony up the extra funds and if the Department would allow him to pay me such an exceptional stipend. That's where we left it. I applied to grad school, and he disappeared back East.

Four months later, I started to twitch about losing my job in Salt Lake. I applied to lots of places, and got a good number of interviews; but all the interest was in places far from home: Thousand Oaks, California; Albuquerque, New Mexico; San Diego; Corvallis, Oregon; Colorado Springs.

Sometime in April, five months after hearing I'd have to change jobs, I got a letter from Cornell University: I had been accepted for admission to the Electrical Engineering Ph.D. Program. About a week later, I got a letter from Prof. Frey. The Department had approved of him paying me what I'd demanded and his sponsor went along with the idea. All other options were off the table now: Carla and I were convinced that I was going to get my Ph.D. at Cornell, and go somewhere afterward to be a professor. My boss, Kent, was happy about this: he felt I'd flourish at Cornell; but flounder in his new job for me.

Just days after these events, I had my monthly lunch with Pastor Stewart. We sat at the very same table in Ruth's Diner where we'd talked, some five months earlier, about my job changing. David, in his typical fashion, sat rock-still, and virtually expressionless as I told him what had transpired. We had not talked of the matter even once since our earlier discussion. As I wrapped up my tale, saying, "Well, it looks like we're moving to Ithaca, New York and I'm going to Cornell to be a grad student."

David's eyes opened wide with amazement. He had forgotten our earlier talk; but now he remembered. "God told me last fall that you were going to come to me and tell me you were going to Cornell!" At that moment, Ruth's Diner became Holy Ground.

A few weeks later, I finished my Master's Degree in Electrical Engineering. We sold a large amount of our stuff and packed what remained in a trailer which I pulled from Salt Lake City to Ithaca. Carla flew ahead with the boys. With a feeling of God's blessings, we were embarked on a huge new phase of our lives.

PART THREE

PILLAR OF PEACE

Ithaca is quite hot in July. We moved into an apartment complex by the highway and we roasted. We also found a great little local fellowship, Asbury Church, in Lansing, just four miles north of our place. The people were very welcoming and there were almost no other students. At the time, I didn't know that Cornell University was founded by the die-hard atheist, Ezra Cornell, to be an atheist institution. He'd become wealthy as the founder and owner of Western Union Telegraph Company in the mid-19th century, and built the university in Ithaca because it was literally the only place in America where anybody would sell him land—knowing he wished to build this monument to his anger towards the Almighty. Even when we arrived there in 1983, there were about 17,000 students, with 30 in Campus Crusade for Christ and 20 in Inter-Varsity Christian Fellowship...Believers were few and far between. Asbury Church was a haven of rest, and Pastor Welle was a joy on Sundays.

Our first Sunday afternoon, we got a knock on the door around 3pm. Carla's cousin, Debbie, with her husband,

Gary, whom we hadn't realized lived only an hour away, somehow found out we were there and came to welcome us to the hinterlands of New York. We were overjoyed. We also didn't know that Gary was pastor of a non-denominational church in Hall, New York. They had three beautiful kids who connected well with our young tots. We love them.

Staying well into the evening, we recounted our marvelous tale of how we came to Ithaca and how I came to Cornell. Gary remarked at the time, "God confirmed in so many miraculous ways that you should be here. Did He really need to go to that length to get you to come?" I hadn't ever thought of it. But I would.

Cornell is not an easy graduate school. I thought I was a good student at the University of Utah. At this Ivy League shrine, however, I was surrounded by geniuses. Among them, I was rather ho-hum. We had celebrities like Carl Sagan teaching classes and multiple Nobel laureates giving special lectures. It was heady and humbling. And hard. No more top of the Dean's List for Charlie. After nine months of heading straight to campus after my breakfast at 7, and coming home in time for dinner at 7:30, putting the boys to bed, and studying until eleven—no vacations, only Sundays off, and no breaks in the non-stop pressure— I wondered if I could survive it.

In March, Carla and I walked down the street to the store together to buy some things. She put peach ice cream and quart jar of pickles on the counter. The checker smirked and commented, "That's a combination which usually only means one thing." Neither of us had spotted the implication. The clerk was right. We discovered we were expecting.

That was it. I could cope no longer. What was I thinking by pulling up roots and moving to that place? I polished up my resume and started looking for jobs. I got immediate responses, although nothing in Utah, and even some interviews. I was about to pull the trigger on a job in California, when cousin Gary showed up on Sunday afternoon with Debbie and the kids, greeting us with a hearty, "How are you all doing?" I proceeded to sing my song of woe and explain why it was time to pack up and head West. It was hard enough just completing the coursework and trying to initiate my dissertation research; but it would be unimaginable with Carla pregnant, and subsequently attempting to nurture a newborn. Completely unflustered, Gary simply asked, "I recall your dramatic tale a year ago of how Our Father had confirmed, many times over, how you are supposed to be here. Did He change His mind? Suppose that extra measure of confirmation might have been for such a time as this?"

I love Gary. But right at that moment, I'm pretty sure I was more angry at him than loving him. Both Carla and I were slain. We just cried. The real solution was to fall on the mercy of God and stay the course. Gary and Debbie agreed they were in this with us. Other than the seemingly insurmountable uphill climb, I had no viable argument otherwise. Remember?

*Casting all your cares on him, because he cares
about you.*
1 Peter 5:7

My first daughter, Katherine Davis Hunt, was born at 4am on October 22, 1984 and despite the trial, we were elated. My mother-in-law, Maxine, came to be with us for the birth. She was a great blessing and help.

As was our custom, we dedicated Katherine to The Lord the day after she was born. Pastor Welle, who was not accustomed to immediate baby dedications, came to the hospital and agreed to join us in the dedication. It was a warm event, although the staff at Thompkins County Hospital was likely a little taken aback. Welle prayed and prayed, and filled with the Holy Ghost, picked Katherine up, lifted her with both hands as high up as he could, and praised God with a loud voice for this treasured daughter, declaring her as anointed by God to be a Pillar of Peace for all. It was beautiful; but there was some nervousness about what Maxine thought of this, and we dared not glance at the gasping nurses.

Several years later, Carla and I visited her parents, Jim and Maxine, with the kids in Butler, Pennsylvania. It was a great visit, but I was uncomfortable when Maxine started to berate one of Carla's siblings for not having had their kids baptized. Maxine was Catholic. After the tensions dissipated and things went on to other matters, Carla approached Maxine and said, "Mom. We haven't had our kids baptized." Max looked bewildered.

"Well, if that thing in the hospital didn't do the trick, I don't know what will!"

SHAKING THE PRESIDENT'S HAND

One interesting Cornell tradition is that the annual graduation ceremony is held in the blistering heat, in the football stadium, led in great pomp and ceremony by the president of the university. Among the numerous degrees being conferred, all of the doctoral recipients march across the stage and the president personally shakes their hand in congratulations. During my stint in Ithaca, the president of Cornell was the eminent Dr. Frank Rhodes, a famous British scholar.

I have mixed feelings about this type of graduation ceremonial stuff. On the one hand, I think it's good to have a landmark here and there in your life to look back on as memorials of achievements. On the other hand, I think it can be a touch arrogant to parade about in ceremonial dress before a crowd, basically saying, "Look at me." I know that our friends and family like to celebrate accomplishments with us, but is this really the best way? I have never been sure. And I take note of the apostle Peter's exhortation and feel a need to check myself:

Humble yourselves, therefore, under the mighty hand of God, so that he may exalt you at the proper time.
1 Peter 5:6

Early in my time at Cornell, I felt insecure that I was qualified to be there and I worried that I would fail and let my family down. Carla and I talked a good deal about this. She firmly decided to stand with whatever I chose to do. She would support that decision.

We pray and look for His guidance. But that doesn't mean it's easy. Especially when our emotions are involved, it's probable our judgement will be clouded.

I'm don't generally remember many dreams I've had. And there are only a few dreams which I would claim were dreams given to me by God.

> *After this I will pour out my Spirit on all humanity;*
> *then your sons and your daughters will prophesy,*
> *your old men will have dreams, and your young*
> *men will see visions.*
> Joel 2:28

One night, I had a vivid dream in which I walked up to Dr. Frank Rhodes and shook his hand. This could only mean one thing. I told Carla this dream in the morning, and we agreed that this was a confirmation that God would help me finish my studies at Cornell, receive my degree, and we would go on to the next stage of life, whatever that might be.

One weekend, over a year later, I was at the JC Penny department store, looking at shirts, and I glanced across the rack and noticed Dr. Frank Rhodes checking out shirts on the same rack. I leaned over to Carla and whispered, "Do you know who that is? That's Frank Rhodes!"

Her response was immediate: "Whatever you do, don't go over there and shake his hand!" I didn't shake it that day; but I did about a year later. God has always been faithful.

PART FOUR

THE GIANT SNOWBALL

Our family has traveled to a lot of places and lived in diverse locations thanks to my job as a Professor at UC Davis. In winter 1990, we spent a few months on assignment in Burlington, Vermont. This is a delightful place; but has its own thermal challenges in winter. Interestingly, we were able to rent a condo in Bolton Valley, a ski resort close to my work assignment at IBM. We all loved it and the kids learned to ski and enjoyed playing in the snow; which is less common for most Californians.

My very independent, seven-year-old, Eddie, was playing in the snowbanks surrounding our home when I got home one evening. It was twilight, and there was just enough light for me to go outside and retrieve firewood from the woodpile for the evening. I asked where Eddie was, and Carla suggested I call him in, considering how cold it gets when the sun goes down at Bolton Valley.

In front of our condo, off to one side, was a 30-foot mountain of ice and snow piled up over the season by the ski resort's snowplows. Walking past the mound of snow, heading back inside with my load of wood, I called out but got no response from my son. I figured he'd gone to the Rec Room across the parking lot, or somewhere else. Bolton Valley is a very safe place and I figured that after dumping off the wood inside, I'd be able to scout around for him.

For no obvious reason, before going inside, I felt like I ought to set down the wood by the door and go over to the snow pile and call again. I went over and yelled out, "Eddie!" No answer. I turned to go back to our place and put the wood away, when I instead felt strangely compelled to check out the massive pile of snow and ice laid out before me. Although there was no daylight left, I saw a strange pair of branches poking out of the ice about halfway up the pile, maybe fifty feet away. They moved slightly, and I thought I heard a sound, like a gentle cry, coming from that direction.

I bolted up the slope of junky snow and ice and discovered the "branches" were a pair of protruding legs. The boy attached to those legs was buried by a six-foot snowball which he'd been playing with. The ice/snowball had been too heavy for him and rolled back downwards towards him; but in his efforts to run away, he tripped on the ice and the snowball pinned him in the center of his back, with only his legs protruding. He would have suffocated, except that in falling forward his face lodged squarely in a boot-print in the snow, providing a tiny air pocket. He couldn't budge and was almost knocked unconscious. In his fright, he vomited into the boot-print. He was stuck.

It's amazing how panic can make us superhuman. I picked up and tossed the half-ton snowball aside. Picking up my completely limp boy, I raced back inside to a very-surprised family. Carla and I were able to revive him and get his body temperature back up. By bedtime, he was okay. Had I gone inside to stack the wood or gone over to the Rec Room, this story would have a very different ending. Our hearts were flooded with awe of how Our Father had intervened to save Eddie's life.

See to it that you don't despise one of these little ones, because I tell you that in heaven their angels continually view the face of my Father in heaven.
Matthew 18:10

MY FATHER IN HEAVEN

I grew up in California; first in Berkeley, and during high school in the Mother Lode town of Sutter Creek (population: 1200). My mother took me to church, St. Clement's Episcopal Church in Berkeley, and later to Trinity Episcopal Church in Sutter Creek. She was a staunch attendee, but my father only went on holidays or special occasions. When I was sixteen, I stopped going because I wasn't a Christian and I didn't see anything spiritual which I wanted at my mother's church. As I grew up, I noticed my father, who had been raised in a strict Baptist home, was actually hostile towards religion, and specifically towards Christianity. In his later years, he jokingly described himself as a retired Buddhist.

After I first went to college, I learned my father's story from stray conversations. When he graduated from high school in Elgin, Illinois in 1930, Dad immediately left home for Chicago. Despite being only sixteen, he wanted to be out of the house, on his own, and not having to live under his parents' Baptist rules. He also clearly didn't like the house rule to attend their church every Sunday. He considered himself done with Jesus. By all reports, my grandparents were actually very nice people: fair, considerate, and loving. So I never could understand the acrimony my Dad carried towards faith, and the Christian faith in particular.

When I accepted Jesus in 1974, I promptly announced my faith to my parents. Despite being a "good Episcopalian," my mother responded with some skepticism. Her analysis of what had happened in my life was that she also had her "religious phase" back in college, but I should realize that my new-found zeal would wear off after a while. She was wrong. My father, however, was profoundly rattled. He took virtually every chance he could to either take sarcastic swipes at my faith, or to argue, quite unconvincingly, about his perceptions of the errors in Christianity. I didn't stop mentioning Jesus to Dad; I made it a priority to pray for him. I prayed that God would save his soul.

Over the years, the hostility towards Jesus amplified in my dad. He made some pretty strong frontal attacks on me, my brother and his wife, and later my wife and my friends. Sometimes, I didn't have a good answer for him. Although faith in Jesus is solidly reasonable, it's not very likely that an unbeliever will forsake a life of sin and follow Jesus because of logical arguments or rational convictions. A person has to want Jesus. A person has to experience the need for Jesus in their soul. When an individual accepts Jesus, we say they have received Him into their heart. The Holy Spirit comes into a person and that person passes from death unto life. This is a supernatural happening. In most cases, these things are the consequence of spiritual events in a person's life; not intellectual conclusions.

One night, I had a dream. In the dream, we were worshipping in The Order of the Lamb. That fellowship held its meetings in the round, with an open area in the middle, where sometimes we might dance or just raise our hands to God in praise. One down side of this format was that any time somebody entered or exited, the entire congregation was distracted by seeing this motion in and out. In the dream, I sat on my chair in the front row, worshiping. The door of the room opened, and I glanced over, only to see my father walking in. He walked straight over to me and sat in the empty chair next to me. He looked at me with a smile, and silently raised his hands to join in worship. My astonished gaze turned towards Heaven, and I worshipped along with him.

I had only been a Believer for 3-4 years at that point, but I took this dream to be a message from God: my father would become a Christian. I prayed all the more and doubled my efforts to share my faith with Dad. The response was not good. He doubled down with some hefty swipes. For example, he noted that his father, who had been a watchmaker back in Elgin, had Parkinson's Disease from 1934 until his death in 1953.

My dad asked, "Look. My parents were clean-living, faithful and devout in their church their whole lives. If this god of yours is so good and so loving, how come he let my father waste away for nineteen years, shaking without any medical treatments? Why did my mother have to suffer and watch the man she loved decay into a cripple requiring her constant care, day and night? Huh?"

I was dumbfounded. I couldn't say a word. I put Dad's question before the Lord, but it wasn't until years later that He answered me, *If your dad asked his mother that same question, she would have responded, 'God has only blessed us our whole lives.' She never complained.*

Another time, sitting at my dad's dinner table with Carla, I was speaking about Jesus. Dad had lost Mom at that point, and he was increasingly anxious about the fact that when I joined The Order of the Lamb, I'd dropped out of college, against my mother's wishes.

In the middle of my preaching about Jesus, Dad cut me off with a curt, "I don't know a lot about Christianity; but one thing I do know is that Christians are supposed to keep their word. You promised your mother, while she was still with us, that you would go back to college and get your degree. But that never happened. So don't talk to me about Jesus until you decide to keep your promises!"

Cut to the heart. That conversation was over. Later that evening, Carla pointed out, "He got you on that one." It was only months later that I returned to the university. Thanks, Dad.

As the years wore on, I became discouraged. Dad's attitude about Jesus only hardened. I rarely prayed for him anymore. On those rare occasions when I spoke about the Faith, the response was swift, blunt, and bitter. I lost hope that my dream was from God. I didn't even think of it for fifteen years.

When Christmas 1993 came, I took all the kids to Salt Lake City to see my brother and sister there, and to go skiing. It was a fun time. As we were about to return, on New Year's Day 1994, I received a phone call telling me that Dad was in the hospital in Stockton, and things looked serious. We drove home fast.

We discovered that Dad had esophageal cancer. It had spread all over his body, and the doctor attending him told me bluntly that he was not likely to live long. I was stricken. The whole family gathered around him and tried our best to comfort him. He knew the prognosis and was accepting it. I committed to drive, each day, to Stockton from our home in Davis, about one hour each way, and visit him. I prayed for him, but it was a bitter prayer. I didn't want to lose my father.

A friend from our church in Davis, Dick Lindholtz, who like my dad, was a veteran of the Second World War, offered to join my family after church to visit Dad. It was Sunday, January 9, 1994. Our pastor, Jeff Chapman, also offered to come. I was thankful for the support; these were tough times. We got to the room at St. Joseph's Hospital, and all my kids, Carla, my brother John, as well as Dick and Jeff, gathered around his bed. Dad looked surprised by the crowd.

After introducing the unexpected guests, Pastor Jeff was direct and quick to speak up. "You're going to die very soon, Ed. God wants you to make up your mind and accept His Son, Jesus. This could be your very last chance. We're here, hoping you'll make that right choice, before it's eternally too late."

Dad looked around the room with wild eyes. My thoughts were quick, *Oh boy. This is not going to be pretty*. But Dick immediately joined in, "Ed, you don't know me. But we're not here to pass the plate. We're here because we love Charlie and Carla and your kids. And because we love them, and because we love God, we love you. Now you and I, we fought on the same battlefields. We're cut from the same bolt of cloth. Your pride won't impress anybody and isn't going to do you a lick of good if you die and go to hell. I'm here to ask you plainly if you want to lay down that pride, accept Jesus, and live with your family forever. He'll accept you, even now, if you'll just ask Him. What do you say?"

More wild eyes. They settled on Dick. He calmed down and said, "Yes. I do want to accept Him." I was stunned. We all were.

We dropped to our knees around Dad in the bed. Dick led him in a deep prayer of repentance and salvation. We cried. We rejoiced. I leaned over the bed to hug my dad. "I love you, Dad."

But eleven-year-old Eddie, ever the hugger, did one better. He climbed right into the bed, wrapped his arms around Dad, and said so softly, "I love you, Granddaddy."

With a gentle pat on the back, Dad replied, "I love you too, Eddie." His namesake was the closest.

Pastor Jeff told Dad that he would join me each day to the hospital to visit and Dad liked that. We did that together, sharing our amazement over the faithfulness of Our Father. It was clear He had struck fertile soil in my dad's heart.

The following Sunday, though, Jeff told me, "I can't go with you today. There's something which has come up. Please tell your dad that I really apologize, and I will be there with you tomorrow."

I got to the room and I was alone with Dad. At this point, he was drifting in and out of dementia. He laid there with his eyes closed; unresponsive. I sat and talked with him anyway. I told him what the Raiders score was. I talked about the kids. I told him about Jeff and apologized for him not being there. No response. I got up and started for the door.

"Oh, what's the use. You don't even know who Jeff Chapman is!"

His voice spoke from behind me, "I know who Jeff Chapman is." I was surprised to hear anything; but, considering his recent lack of lucidity, I wasn't very convinced of what he had said.

"Oh yeah? Who is Jeff Chapman?"

"He's the man who convinced me to do what I'd told myself I would never do."

"What's that, Dad?"

"Talk to God."

I was cut to the bone. I remember thinking, "Move over, Dad. I need to lie down too."

Five days later, a nurse called our house at 5am. "Your father is dead." I drove to St. Joseph's. The same hospital where my mother had died eighteen years earlier. I walked into the room. His body lay there like stone, face up, eyes closed. I'd never seen a dead person before. I could see so clearly: he wasn't there anymore. My dream had come true. His spirit had departed. My father had gone to be with Jesus.

THE THREE PALMS

Carla had grown up in rural Western Pennsylvania, and I'd gone through high school in the Sierra foothills. We both loved the country, and had always wanted to live where we could have horses, and enjoy the outdoors. But country property in California, even in the deserts and the outbacks, is unaffordable. We looked at country homes many times; but always went away discouraged. There was no way we could afford a home for our family in the country.

At one point, Carla told me, "I don't want to look at properties anymore. I just get discouraged. I want to give up. I want to move away to someplace else." We stopped visiting the places for sale around Davis and just accepted the facts. Wasn't going to happen.

I was driving alone across town one Sunday in early 1995, and stopped to look at an Open House. It wasn't actually a place I'd likely want to move into, so I'm not sure what prompted me to stop. Maybe the cookies they gave away. The realtor, a very amiable, smiling fellow named Don, greeted me. Even though he quickly realized this house wasn't our cup of tea, he soon discovered what we really wanted. He also proclaimed that the house we did have, a 70s-era

Suburbia Special, was just the kind of place folks wanted, and in a very desirable neighborhood. If we ever want help finding our dream, or selling our city home, he's our man.

Carla started to have dreams. In her dreams, she envisioned her country home. It was old and rustic, and had high ceilings with high, old-fashioned baseboards. The kids played everywhere. It had a barn with horses, and she rode through the fields with her friends and family. It felt like home. She told me of her dream; but I wasn't sure what to make of all this. I wished I could help make her dream come true.

In May, the following year, I saw a picture in the Friday Real Estate section of our local paper. There was this old, somewhat frumpy farmhouse. It was an estate sale by the university. For sale, as is, where is, by sealed bid. A two-hour public viewing of the place was scheduled for a week later, and that was to be the only time to visit the place. I showed the picture to Carla at dinner. "Hmmm. I could look at that." So we went.

The long driveway was lined with cars, and there were a hundred or so people checking the place out. We quietly walked from our car, parked at the end of the road, down to the house, with its three giant palm trees majestically planted in front. We went up the stairs, and walked in.

Carla took one step in and stopped. She looked up at the ceiling, looked down at the baseboards and immediately said, "This is my house!" *Huh?* "This is the house in my dreams. Remember? I told you about this place."

I was struck stupid. She didn't do more than glance in a room or two as she walked down the long hall to the dining room where she found a university agent handing out bid packages. After taking one, she looked at the lady and said, "You might as well stop handing these out. I can tell you right now: this is my house."

The agent smirked at her and continued handing out packages. Carla and I left without really looking the place over much. No need to. This is all the more striking when you consider that Carla is not a very impulsive person.

Nobody slept that night. We contacted friends from church and invited them over. He was a local real-estate agent. We told him our dream of wanting to buy the Three Palms, Carla's dream house. "Yeah. You and half of Davis. No way you'll ever get into that house using the equity from this place." He glanced about with obvious contempt. Our hearts sank.

I brought over a good friend, Walt, who I knew was a very savvy investor, specializing in real estate. I showed him the pictures and the bid package. We shared our dream. Walt looked at me with love and understanding, but also with the face of pragmatic reality.

"Charlie. Love your wife; not your home. I don't think that place will sell. A cash deal, 'as is', without even a bug report or structural inspection? Nobody but a rich idiot would go for that. And no bank would give a mortgage on it. It's nothing but an unrealistic risk."

Squashed dreams can be very painful. When the bids went in, a few weeks later, we didn't include one. We couldn't. Carla and the kids went back to Pennsylvania, to the grandparents', for the summer, and I went to Stuttgart on a research project. We let it go and tried to forget.

When we got back to Davis in late summer, I went to lunch with a friend downtown and spotted John Yates, the university's Director of Business Relations. We were acquaintances, so I went over to say hi and asked, "So who got the old property on the west side of town?"

He looked surprised, and replied, "Well, nobody. Six bids; but not one of them met the University's rules. Frankly, I was surprised you, with that gaggle of kids you have, didn't bid on it."

I related what Walt had said, and told him I couldn't afford such risk. "Well, then. What do we need to do to get it sold? According to state regulations, we're not allowed to hang onto it."

My opinion was simple: get the house up to code; get an engineering report verifying its structural worthiness; get a pest report and fix any problems so a bank could pre-approve a bid. What I didn't know was that the Three Palms, being built in 1868, was on the registry of the Historical Society. What I'd suggested was no small matter. Even so, within weeks, John took my words to heart, and a new bid was opened. All deficiencies were fixed, and the 150-page engineering report proclaimed that the house and barn were so well built that the rest of Yolo County would collapse around this house. The stage was set.

The problem was *How do we do this?* Our house wasn't worth very much, we had debts and a pre-approval seemed unlikely. We didn't have sufficient cash to put down the surety deposit. I remembered my smiling Realtor, Don, at the open house a year or two earlier and gave him a call.

Like a breath of fresh air and with oozing optimism, Don proclaimed, "Do exactly what I say, and I'll get you into that house!" And so we followed his instructions, to the letter. We sold our cars, with their car payments, and bought clunkers with the cash. We disposed of every debt we could with the exception of our home mortgage. We borrowed cash from my siblings to make the security deposit and the down payment. Our house went on the market. We put in our bid package, pledging the highest possible amount we figured I could qualify to get a mortgage for.

Don was meticulous in assuring that we met every one of the university's numerous rules for the bid, including "No contingencies." If we failed to finance the purchase, we'd lose our surety deposit (15% of the bid, in cash.) They were sealed bids; but we learned there were six of them.

On October 13, 1996, they opened the bids and a smiling Don emerged from the bid session, triumphantly proclaiming, "You won the bid!"

Carla was right. This *is* her house. We learned that the other bids, again, didn't qualify. The highest bid was actually $45,000 more than ours, and was made by Mark, a friend from our church, who is a lawyer. Lawyers can't abide with a "no contingencies" clause. Mark had included a statement, on letterhead, citing the California law which disallowed such a clause in the bid rules, and proclaimed that he would sue if they disallowed his contingencies. His bid got tossed; and sue he did.

I heard later, though, that Mark's wife intervened with something like, "Really, Honey. You're going to sue the university over the Hunts' winning the bid? With all those little kids?" The suit got quickly dropped.

We moved in on Thanksgiving Day. There wasn't even a working stove yet; but a crowd of fifty or so of our friends from church came out to rejoice with us. Everybody explored the property, with the barn, the workshop, the farm-worker's shack, the greenhouse and all, from edge to edge. The place was a dump, but it was our dump now. We eventually all stood on the Widow's Walk on the roof, facing all four directions, looking out on our 9-acre home that God had given us. We all raised our hands to heaven, reaching out in all directions and claimed the Three Palms for the Lord. We dedicated the place to Him and His Glory, and prayed together that He would always bless the old house, protect it with his angels, and bless those who come there. He has answered that prayer, and we always thank Him for our beautiful home.

THE STING OF A LIFETIME

On a glorious autumn day in November 2000, I scheduled a lunch date with Carla. Riding my bike across the UC Davis campus, I felt a falling oak leaf land in my hair and I tried to brush it away. It was not a leaf. It was a wasp. And it responded to my brushing with a frontal assault on my left hand's middle finger. I shook my hand hard and got rid of the insect, but found myself quite out of control riding the bike. With my left hand on fire, I grabbed the brake with all I had. I stopped to regain my composure and then rode on to lunch.

My dear wife was the picture of compassion when I told her my story. After looking at my left hand, though, she was more concerned about the angle of my middle finger than the welts from the multiple stings. "That's definitely not right. You need to go to the doctor and get that looked at." It was clear something was goofy: if I put my hand flat on the table, my middle finger poked out, involuntarily, about thirty degrees to the left, pushing aside my ring and little fingers. I agreed to get it looked at.

After lunch, I called my doctor. I'm a healthy person, and I rarely go to the doctor. But this physician was more than my "Primary Care Physician." He was my dear friend from church, Lance, with whom I have shared many spiritual and family experiences. He had long before given me his private number, which I'd never called until then.

Much to my surprise, Lance was quick to say, "Come over now. I want to see this." Even more surprising was to go right into the office, have him glance at my hand, and have him say, "I've never in all my career seen anything like this." Glancing at his watch, he followed by saying, "But I know who likely has. The best hand surgeon in Northern California is in the next office, and we might be able to catch her if we run right over."

We went through the back doors of the doctors' offices and thankfully caught our trusty expert right as she was leaving for the day. She took a quick glance at my hand and immediately said, "Oh my. I've only seen this four times in my life before. You have torn the hood which holds your extensor tendon on the back of your middle finger. This needs to be repaired immediately or you'll lose the proper function of that finger, permanently. Go to the front desk and tell my staff I said you need to be an add-on to tomorrow's surgical schedule. Then, go home and put this on ice." With that, she bolted out the door.

I had not imagined I'd be at the hospital the next day. But there I was, the seventeenth procedure my surgeon would perform that day. I was put under general anesthesia, and after a mere twenty minutes of surgery, I was wheeled out to the recovery room. I also had not imagined six months of subsequent recovery and physical therapy was ahead. To this day, my hand functions perfectly.

This chain of events saved my guitar hand. I have played guitar for fifty years, and most of that time my primary musical passion has been to lead worship. Had I not had lunch with Carla and been urged to go to the doctor; had I not gotten Lance's private number; had Lance not been available and willing to see me right then; had it been any other doctor, who likely would have scheduled me for a specialist weeks later; had we not caught this magic hand surgeon before she walked out; had we not gotten the last slot on the surgery schedule for the next day: things in my life since that day would have been very different. We sometimes don't see the miracle right before us in plain view. A large group of seemingly ordinary events, in this case, formed a chain which, for me, is an overwhelming demonstration of God's love and care.

A DARK DAY BEHIND THE BARN

Our wonderful home, *The Three Palms*, is graced with a magnificent, 115-year-old, 7,800 square foot redwood barn which is several hundred yards behind our house. Besides being the "Horsey Hilton" in the winter, it's been "Barnyard Theatre" for over a decade of summers, as well as the venue of many musical concerts, and even my son Ed's wedding. It's a place where people have often gone, for any number of reasons, even when we're not home. For my family, and many others, it's a special place.

One day, two folks I know decided to visit the barn during the day. I wasn't home. This man and woman found themselves out behind the barn, alone.

Interestingly, my longtime friend and Brother in The Lord, Dave, who I'd known since before The Order of The Lamb days, was driving through Davis that day. He lives up in the foothills East of Sonora, and rarely passes our way; but this day he decided to pay a visit. Not finding anybody home, instead of going on his way back to Sonora, he felt led to take a hike out to the barn. Dave is not particularly interested in barnyard animals. Why would he go out to the barn?

He walked around to the back of the barn and turned the corner at the very instant that the two visitors were commencing in passionate activity. They were not happy to see Dave. He had met both before and knew that they were married. But not to each other.

This awkward moment became the catalyst for a long sequence of ensuing events: confession, repentance, counseling, reconciliation, and restoration in faith; both to their own spouses and to The Lord. This happened decades ago; but to this day, with new life and renewal, their fidelity remains to the partners to whom they had each respectively vowed their lives.

THE HOLY MOUNTAIN

"Do not come any closer," God said.
"Take off your sandals, for the place where you are
standing is holy ground."
Exodus 3:5

It was clear to Moses and it's clear to me: there are places in this world which are quite special. They are holy ground, and God visits His people in these places at times.

In early 2002, in the wake of losing our oldest daughter to state custody, due to her struggles with bipolar disorder, our family was at risk. Counselors, both for Carla and for me, warned that recovery from the fallout of this type of family trauma is very difficult. Our chances to survive as a couple, and as a family, were less than fifty percent, according to the statistics.

At the university, I had earned a one-year sabbatical, and research collaborators at the University of Barcelona invited me to join their faculty for a year. The counselors, to our surprise, encouraged us to accept the invitation. Get away from the scene of our trials. Gather our other children close and spend more time with them. Embrace a new environment and experience new things. So, that Fall, off we went.

This was a wonderful, healing year. We experienced many new things. We made memories and friends for a lifetime. And we refocused our relationships, as a family and as Believers in Jesus. We fellowshipped, in English, at The International Church of Barcelona: they warmly welcomed us and helped us heal as a family.

Barcelona is in Catalonia, at the northeast corner of the Iberian Peninsula. About sixty miles northwest of the City is the mountain of Montserrat. This is a strange-looking, rocky protrusion which has long been regarded as a special place to meet God. There is an ancient, active monastery near the top. There is a beautiful church with a special school for boys. This is the place where Ignatius de Loyola, the founder of the Jesuits, had his first major experience with God in the sixteenth century. He lived as a hermit near there for over a year and wrote his famous book, *Spiritual Exercises*, which remains today as a focal guide for Christian retreats. It is loved by both Catholics and Protestants alike.

For our anniversary, Carla and I went alone to Montserrat and stayed at the modest hotel there for two days. Despite the good things we'd experienced so far in our year in Catalonia, we still wrestled with the recovery process. Although I don't have much affinity for Roman Catholic rituals, I found the evening vespers were striking and moving. While I went, Carla stayed in the hotel enjoying quiet time. I knew God was calling me to a deeper commitment to Him.

Look, I have refined you, but not as silver;
I have tested you in the furnace of affliction.
Isaiah 48:10

Returning to Barcelona and the kids, we both felt changed. On the train, Carla spoke up and told me, "While you were at vespers, God came and visited me." She explained that The Spirit gave her a vision of how our marriage is like the keep of a castle. The keep sits as the most secure place in the castle. Only the lord and lady of the castle can go in there when a siege is on. Everything outside may be chaos; but in the keep is safety. We returned to Barcelona, and later to California, knowing we'd been to a Holy Mountain of God, and that He had visited us there to protect us, to heal us, and to bind us to each other.

We all, with unveiled faces, are looking as in a mirror
at the glory of the Lord and are being transformed into
the same image from glory to glory; this is from the
Lord who is the Spirit.

2 Corinthians 3:18

THE MESSENGER IN THE AIRPORT

*God is our refuge and strength, a helper who is
always found in times of trouble.*
Psalm 46:1

*My God sent his angel and shut the lions' mouths;
and they haven't harmed me...*
Daniel 6:22

Despite many struggles, our oldest daughter, Katherine, overcame her neuro-biological disorder and was able to graduate from high school and attend college in San Diego, where she did well. She also started to learn to manage her disease and started to develop a support network around her in case things got tough. She fought admirably. During that time, though, she did not want to have anything to do with me and very little with Carla. She rarely returned home, except for a few, short visits. For me, this was painful.

One afternoon I was sitting at my desk at work. It was right before the Memorial-Day weekend and the phone rang. "Hello. This is Dr. Smith at Sunset-Valley Psychiatric Hospital in San Diego. Do you have a daughter named Katherine?"

I was alarmed. He went on to explain that Katherine had been involuntarily admitted to the hospital, having a psychotic episode. She had somehow been able to leave the hospital against doctors' orders and they were unable to locate her. They were afraid she could be in great danger to herself, due to her present condition.

"Do you know how to find her?" I did not. But I called Carla, who did know some of Katherine's friends, and I urged her to fly immediately to San Diego and look for our daughter. Carla dropped everything and went.

After an anxious day or two, Carla finally located Katherine and was shocked to be greeted with, "What are you doing here?"

"The hospital said you were in trouble, and they needed help finding you."

"Go away. I don't want you here. How dare they violate confidentiality and contact you!"

Carla felt crushed with rejection. She called me and we spoke for some time. I urged her to head straight for the airport and catch the next flight home to the rest of her family. She should come home to where she was loved and wanted. I could see no way she could help Katherine at that point. Carla left right away for Lindbergh Field.

Southwest Airlines has hourly flights from San Diego to Sacramento, and if there is space, they will allow you to switch to a flight you're not booked for, on a stand-by basis. We had not considered the Memorial-Day weekend travel crunch. All flights were full, and so Carla sat in the waiting area for the Sacramento flights, hoping for a cancelled reservation to open. She felt overwhelmed and dejected. From her mobile phone, she called me and let me know it might be some time.

Later, I called to check in. I also hoped to encourage her. She answered her phone and you could hear the loud clatter of the waiting area. "Believe it or not, I'm right in the middle of praying with a lady."

Immediately, my heart pounded with the realization: this is an angel. All I could say was, "Call me back when you're able." Click.

Later, I learned what was transpiring. The waiting area had almost no seats available; but Carla found one. Soon, an oddly-dressed, friendly middle-aged woman, weighted down with her carry-on stuff, plopped herself down right next to Carla and started right in: "Are you going to Sacramento to visit family? I'm on this next flight."

Carla didn't really want to talk; but did say she had seen family in San Diego and was now heading home. After a few seconds, the lady turned to her and said, "Your daughter is going to be all right. God is going to restore what was lost." She proceeded to tell Carla that the Lord was with her. She should not be afraid. The benevolent woman spoke with authority about several things which had transpired in the previous days.

How did this stranger know anything about the situation? Carla hadn't even told her we have a daughter, or that anything had gone wrong. She sat there stunned at what she was hearing, when the lady said, "Let's pray together right now."

Right there in the noise and clamor they held hands and sought Our Father together. That's when Carla's phone rang, with me inquiring about her well-being. After I hung up, they went right back to praying. Carla said that the weight of the world was lifted off her shoulders. Peace. Confidence in God. Hope for the future. No airport waiting area ever was so comforting and filled with light. "Katherine is called by God and she is going to be okay." How did this woman know our girl's name?

After they prayed, Carla asked the lady to watch her bag so she could run to the rest room. Since it was some time before the next flight would commence boarding, the lady said it was no trouble. When Carla returned in a few minutes, she found her bag just sitting there, and her benevolent comforter nowhere in sight. She asked the person who had been sitting on the stranger's other side, "Did you see where the lady who was sitting here went?"

The unexpected response was, "What lady?"

A bit unnerved, Carla walked to the gate for the flight to Sacramento, which was about to board. She scanned the line of waiting passengers. She wanted to thank her new-found friend. After some time, the flight was fully boarded, the door shut; but Carla never saw her again.

A seat became available on the subsequent flight and I picked up Carla at the Sacramento airport. She was tired and unexpectedly calm. After a long hug, she said, "I think the Lord sent me an angel!" I told her that I had thought the same thing when we'd talked briefly on the phone several hours earlier. We went home in peace.

Don't neglect to show hospitality, for by doing this some have welcomed angels as guests without knowing it.

Hebrews 13:2

HOW NOMA DIED

I have taught Bible studies in a small-group fellowship for years. Noma was a participant for over a decade. She came from a traditional Methodist background, particularly embracing the teachings of John Wesley. She also lived a life of joy mixed with suffering. Her husband, a Methodist minister who died young, as well as one daughter, who lives to this day, suffered from what she called mental illness. Today we would place their maladies among the group of neuro-biological disorders (schizophrenia, bipolar, obsessive-compulsive, clinical depression, etc.) The challenges in her life did not rob her of the joy God had given her: she projected joy and hope wherever she went. And yet, she did endure frustrations.

Even well into her eighties, when she could no longer drive her car but had to rely on the transit in town for elderly people, Noma accepted the circumstances and moved forward. Noma was faithful in her commitments to those she felt God had put in her path. This was her ministry. Small groups, prayer meetings, daily reading and study, and our larger church meetings on Sunday: she was always there.

I relished my conversations with Noma because she was transparent and unafraid to speak her mind to me. If she perceived I had something right or wrong, she told me. She readily discussed her experiences of success and failure she had with her family. Because she knew our experiences, she was particularly available to talk with me about neuro-biological disorders, and all that accompanies them. After she stopped driving, I drove her home after our small-group study each week. These were particularly rich times, albeit relatively short. We trusted each other, and I felt she was a gift God had placed in my path: a wise Sister who could teach me a great deal.

One fellowship Noma always participated in, with her daughter Charlotte, was a women's meeting on Tuesdays, in the afternoon. Not long ago, Charlotte was surprised to go to the meeting and not find Noma there. She called her, but got no answer. Afterward, she went to Noma's house, went in and spotted Noma, her Mom, laid back in her overstuffed reading chair. Her book was laying on her chest, with her hands nestled over it. Her face was tranquil, peaceful. "Oh, here we go again. Mom has fallen asleep while reading." But she wasn't asleep: Charlotte quickly discovered that Noma wasn't there.

The representative from the coroner's office came and examined everything. He noted there'd been no heart attack or stroke. No health problem or struggle. Noma had paused in her reading, laid down her book, and then her body stopped. Noma had gone home.

WAS BLIND BUT NOW I SEE

I started wearing glasses when I was a junior in high school. Since then, I've had various degrees of correction for nearsightedness in both eyes. For the last forty years, I have been unable to read without my glasses, and in the last decade I've worn bifocals.

On May 18th, 2018, I went to donate blood, which has been my practice every eight weeks for over fifteen years. I'm a generally healthy person, and I've always had great blood pressure, low cholesterol, and low lipids; it's been rare for me to be sick. But that Friday, the blood folks would not allow me to donate because my blood pressure was too high. I was surprised. It had never been high before. The nurse was pretty low-key about it.

She assured me this was likely a transient spike, and on another day it could be normal again. "Maybe you drank too much coffee this morning, or had a fight with your wife, or had some stressful event." I'd had none of that. She suggested I check my pressure every day or two for a couple of weeks, and if it didn't go down, go see my doctor. That's where I left it.

Two days later, my vision became somewhat blurry. I figured this was due to high dust, pollen, and pesticides in the air. But on Monday and Tuesday, things got worse. By Tuesday night, I could not focus my right eye at all. At music rehearsal that night, I couldn't read my sheet music, and my band partners were bold to say, "You need to see a doctor about this."

The next day, Wednesday, I went to a clinic in Livermore, where the doctor stated that although my blood pressure was high, it was not alarming; however, the sudden inability to focus my right eye was worthy of a visit to the optometrist. On that advice, I went the very next day, Thursday.

Dr. Mark, my optometrist, and I knew each other for years: our kids grew up together, and we are both soccer enthusiasts. I had a vision checkup just four months earlier. This time, he measured a slight change in my left eye; but a serious loss of vision in my right eye. He wasted no words: "Go see your doctor soon. This is not an optometric issue, this is a medical problem, and alarming." Mark followed this by letting me know he didn't use the term "alarming" easily.

Walking out of his office, I called my family doctor, who said, "Come in. Now." Which I did. He echoed the optometrist's alarm, saying, "There's about six different things that could be causing this; but, frankly, none of them are good." After calling a few folks, he had me scheduled for a neurologist visit and an ophthalmologist visit the next morning.

I spent 8am to 3pm on Friday in doctors' offices, getting tests. Carla went with me, which was a huge comfort. My band partner, Clyde, who on Tuesday had been proactive to encourage me to seek medical help, agreed to pray, along with his wife, Katie, over the course of the day. We checked in with each other as things progressed. The two specialists jointly scheduled an urgent MRI, which would be performed in a week.

That Friday with the doctors was not a confidence-building experience because the neurologist and ophthalmologist had 180-degree opposite opinions.

One said, "Take massive doses of steroids, starting right now, to mitigate optic nerve neuritis, which is irreversible and will leave your right eye blind. I'll call the pharmacy. You need to stop there on your way home."

The other physician said, "Don't take the steroids. Your blood pressure will spike even higher, and you could have a stroke." I subsequently spoke with both of them, pointing out that their respective recommendations were contradictory.

They both advised, "Do what you feel is best." I know nothing about medicine. I had no basis for forming an opinion. So I called my family doctor's office and was told he had left for the three-day weekend.

In desperation, I called my friend, Andy, who is an orthopedic surgeon, and asked him what he'd do. His advice was, "If your vision gets worse, take the steroid. If it gets better, don't. Continue with the tests and see what the overall issue is." Carla, and I felt confident in Andy's sage advice: that of an MD, a friend, and a Brother in Jesus. No steroids for now, which was fine with me.

I went that Friday evening to worship-music rehearsal. My vision was awful, and I probably should not have been driving. But towards the middle of rehearsal, our leader, Meagan, brought us a new worship song which I'd never heard before and I realized I couldn't even read the music to try to play it. I was distressed. It appeared my vision was worse and so I'd better take the steroids. In anxiety, I tossed my glasses aside, embarrassed to admit I couldn't follow the tune with the rest of the group.

The rest of the team started to play, not realizing I was sitting out. But then, I turned my gaze back to the music chart and was astonished that without my glasses I could read it perfectly. I covered my right eye: my left read it perfectly. I covered my left eye: the right read it perfectly. Opening both, the words and music on the page literally glowed at me with crystal clarity.

I was stunned and confused. I joined in, and we played through the tune. Afterward, unable to contain myself, I raised my hand. Meagan, by that time, was frustrated with several team members because she felt the new tune was not being played the way she hoped. She saw my hand up and said, tersely, "Yeah, Charlie. What do you want?"

With the door open, I said, "This has nothing to do with our music." I told them about my long, exasperating day and about what had just happened. Standing a few feet away, Clyde beamed with joy. We had a great rehearsal, after that.

It was curious, though, that out of nine of us at rehearsal, everybody responded to hearing my story differently. Some worshipped openly. Some expressed great joy. My Tuesday band partner, Clyde, who'd been praying for me, was jubilant that God had restored my vision. Some were vocal to thank God for being with us at rehearsal. Some were quiet and pondering, "What just happened?"

Despite my vision, and blood pressure, being just fine, I did go ahead with the MRI the following week. My family doctor called me and said that inexplicably the results were all normal. I gave him my explanation: "I think God healed whatever was wrong and restored my vision in the process." After a brief pause, Dr. Ewens responded, "I can live with that!"

I had follow-up appointments with the neurologist and the ophthalmologist. The neurologist's office merely cancelled the appointment without comment. The ophthalmologist, though, had her technicians do the same battery of tests they had performed just two weeks earlier. One tech commented, "This is not the result we were expecting to see." I gave her my story, and my view on what had happened. Her response was a brief, "Wow!"

Subsequently, the ophthalmologist came in with my chart. Silently, she put drops in my eyes and looked around my retina and into the optic nerve. After quite a while in silence, she turned away from me, staring at the chart and said, "I have no explanation for what I'm seeing here."

I said, "I think I do!" To that she turned to me and gave a mildly sarcastic reply, "Oh, do tell!" I told her about

Clyde's and Katie's prayers. I told her about the experience at the rehearsal.

I told her, "I think God healed me of whatever was wrong, and restored my vision to 20-20 to confirm to me that it was His doing." The doctor silently stared at me, slowly turned back towards the wall, and finally said, "I think we don't need your next follow-up appointment. Go ahead and cancel it. I encourage you to do as Dr. Ewens said, 'Try to lose twenty-five pounds. Double your exercise. Use less salt.' To which I would add, 'enjoy your 20-20 vision.'"

That was two years ago, as I write this. My vision remains clear. I've not worn my glasses since. (In fact, I had to stop at the store and buy some non-prescription sunglasses.) A few weeks ago, at the Department of Motor Vehicles, I was renewing my license and the agent said, "It says here you need corrective lenses."

I told her, "Not anymore. God restored my vision!" I told her what had happened. She responded, "That's a really good story. But I'll have to give you the eye test." I passed the test with a certain feeling of victory. Interestingly, the cataract in my left eye, which had blurred the center of that eye's vision for a couple of years, also appears to be gone. Nobody had prayed specifically that normal vision be restored for me, or that the cataract would go away; but God chose to do those things. I'll never know why my blood pressure shot up, or why my vision went crazy in my right eye. I am so thankful for His intervention. This is a miracle.

AFTERWORD

I see in the Scriptures that miracles, which are throughout the Bible, are never part of some magic act. Most of God's miracles, we never even see. Our Father brings miracles to our attention in order to teach us, to transform us, and to guide us into what He is doing in this world. So, naturally, it begs the question, *Why did He choose to do this?* On the surface, it could be as simple as to say, "Don't ignore your blood pressure."

Or it could be something that nobody will ever be aware of in this lifetime.

It should not be questioned that Our Father loves each of us, individually. Jesus loves us quite personally. Consider this psalm, among many others:

> *LORD, you have searched me and known me. You know when I sit down and when I stand up; you understand my thoughts from far away. You observe my travels and my rest; you are aware of all my ways. Before a word is on my tongue, you know all about it, LORD. You have encircled me; you have placed your hand on me...Where can I go to escape your Spirit? Where can I flee from your presence? If I go up to heaven, you are there; if I make my bed in Sheol, you are there. If I live at the eastern horizon or settle at the western limits, even there your hand*

will lead me; your right hand will hold on to me. If I say, 'Surely the darkness will hide me, and the light around me will be night'—even the darkness is not dark to you. The night shines like the day; darkness and light are alike to you. For it was you who created my inward parts; you knit me together in my mother's womb. I will praise you because I have been remarkably and wondrously made. Your works are wondrous, and I know this very well. My bones were not hidden from you when I was made in secret, when I was formed in the depths of the earth. Your eyes saw me when I was formless; all my days were written in your book and planned before a single one of them began.
Psalm 139 1-5, 7-16

Or we can simply look at what Jesus said to his disciples:

Indeed, the hairs of your head are all counted. Don't be afraid...
Luke 12:7

And there is what the Apostle said:

No creature is hidden from him, but all things are naked and exposed to the eyes of him to whom we must give an account.
Hebrews 4:13

And John, being commanded to write down the words of Jesus to the churches, plainly wrote:

Let anyone who has ears to hear listen to what the Spirit says to the churches. To the one who conquers, I will give some of the hidden manna.

I will also give him a white stone, and on the stone a new name is inscribed that no one knows except the one who receives it.
Revelation 2:17

It can't get any more intimate than that!

And yet, I am like every other Believer: I am a member of the Church. The larger group of all the over-comers who follow Jesus today. This is a mighty congregation, all over the world, gathered before the throne of God and worshiping Him together. Although my experiences are special and personal to me, I don't perceive myself as being anyone out of the ordinary in that congregation.

The congregation I speak of is not some exclusive club. Jesus wants all of us and He calls to all of us. In the final chapter of the Bible, Jesus says it plainly:

Both the Spirit and the bride say, "Come!" Let anyone who hears, say, "Come!" Let the one who is thirsty come. Let the one who desires take the water of life freely.
Rev 22:17

I hear what He is saying, and I echo His words: Come. Miracles are happening to everyone. I am not the exception. I am the norm. I have learned to look for those miracles because, if I fail to do that, they might go unnoticed. When I see them, I feel a deep sense of thankfulness that God sees me in the crowd, and says, "I love you."

Glory to God.

ABOUT
KHARIS PUBLISHING

KHARIS PUBLISHING is an independent, traditional publishing house with a core mission to publish impactful books, and channel proceeds into establishing mini-libraries or resource centers for orphanages in developing countries, so these kids will learn to read, dream, and grow. Every time you purchase a book from Kharis Publishing or partner as an author, you are helping give these kids an amazing opportunity to read, dream, and grow. Kharis Publishing is an imprint of Kharis Media LLC. Learn more at https://www.kharispublishing.com.